Healing Wisdom
for a Wounded World

My Life-Changing Journey Through a Shamanic School

Book 2

WEAM NAMOU

HERMiZ
PUBLiSHING

Library of Congress Cataloging-in-Publication Data:
2 0 1 6 9 0 0 4 2 6
Namou, Weam

Healing Wisdom for a Wounded World
My Life-Changing Journey Through a Shamanic School
Book 2
(memoir)

ISBN: 978-1-945371-99-8
First Edition

Published in the United States of America by:
Hermiz Publishing, Inc.
Sterling Heights, MI

10 9 8 7 6 5 4 3 2 1

Contents

To my ancestors

Chapter 1
IDLENESS

"Your goal is just to be," said my first year mentor, Leslie, after I finished telling her over the phone that, for the life of me, I could not set any goals for the New Year coming up in a few days. For someone who fell short of meeting last year's deadline of finishing her book, this seemed insane, completely inappropriate, and out of character – although it felt right to just be.

"It is winter, a time for a shaman to rest, to hibernate with the bear and be with your dreams," she said. "Next year you will learn how to move energy. I'm so excited for you."

We chitchatted briefly because I could hardly speak. Stomach flu had me curled up in bed like a puppy. I stared out the window at the evergreen sprinkled with snow, and I felt the whisper of the sunrays that caressed my bedroom. Not making a New Year resolution! Who ever heard of that? This tradition, started by Ancient Babylonians some four thousand years ago, was in my DNA.

For the Babylonians, the first new moon following the vernal equinox, the day in late March with an equal amount of sunlight and darkness, heralded the start of a new year. They made promises to their gods that they would return borrowed objects and pay their debts. They marked the occasion with a massive religious festival called Akitu, derived from the Sumerian word for barley, which was cut in the spring. This festival involved a different ritual on each of its eleven days.

I turned to my husband, who was getting dressed for work, his back against me. He put the green work T-shirt over his tall and lean body, and then he sat at the edge of the bed to put on his socks. I could see from the side of his face the handsome and manly Roman nose, cleft chin, high cheek bones, and moustache which made him look like an Arabian prince. I asked, "Do you remember the last time I stayed in bed all day?"

"When you gave birth to our kids and had to sleep in the hospital," he said.

I returned my gaze to the window and thought, maybe I need the stomach flu. I would never have taken the liberty to fully rest on my own, to unwrap my muscles and stretch and release tension that had gone unnoticed for years. Besides, Babylonians celebrated a new year in late March, which is considered a logical choice for a new year, when spring begins and new crops are planted. January, on the other hand, has no astronomical nor agricultural significance. It is purely random. The Romans continued to observe the New Year on March 25, but their calendar was constantly tampered with by various emperors so that the calendar soon became out of synchronization with the sun. I wondered, had we not tampered with nature's clock, had we synchronized our new resolution with the equinox, would we have better luck keeping resolutions? According to statistics, only eight percent of people will achieve their New Year's resolutions.

February arrived, bringing with it the first quarter school material, called *Face of the Earth Lodge*. I read the study guide, welcoming the messages of how, this year, we will acquire very definite tools for our shamanic work, such as drums, rattles, stones, crystals, talking sticks, and shields. The intent for this year was to understand how to bring form into the world; to experience holding energy and moving it out into the universe; to develop the ability to move energy into objects for healing and sacred work; to learn how to use sacred tools powerfully in a way that doesn't manipulate ourselves or others; to prepare for the building of dreambodies and develop the skills for lucid dreaming.

As I read the first few pages, a switch turned on. I disrobed from the state of torpor, put on a new pair of energy, along with a coat and gloves, and went for a walk. An extra silence filled our subdivision, given the twenty degree temperature, the dark evening hour of six o'clock, and the Super Bowl kickoff scheduled in half an hour. The heavy silence made the occasional dog bark sound as musical as a Beethoven symphony. Light snow and a gentle breeze joined me in this walk, softly stroking my long hair and my face as I thought long, long thoughts about my past.

It seemed that most of what I had set my intent on had somehow or another, at some point in my life, manifested. It is true that our thoughts and actions create the bulk of our reality, though we often forget that. We forget to honor the reality we arrived to, the dream we birthed, and we slip into a worry over the next dream, sadly and foolishly wondering where, when, how, why? Why not surrender to the process the way we do at night, when we rest our heads on the pillow, place the bedsheets over us, close our eyes, and submit to a higher self?

I marched on, my breathing growing louder and deeper, my heart tumbling into a newer determination to continue on the path I had chosen. Suddenly, the sight of lanterns on several peoples' front yards and a few electric candles at one house's window sills caught my attention. Were they there before, and if so, why had I only noticed them now? Their light penetrated into my heart, smiling upon me with their blessings.

At home, my husband and children sat in front of the TV, watching the game. As I removed my coat, layers of snow plopped onto the floor. I wiped the area with a towel then went into my room to read more of the school's study guide. It talked about how, this year, our instructors would prepare us to become a shaman warrior and ready us for battle against our enemies, ignorance, chaos, and negativities, the very things that lead to disease, war, evil, imbalance, and disharmony within us and within nature. It emphasized the importance of being aware of everything we think and do. It said that in order for a woman to take her power in the world, her voice needs to be heard, and that the tasks we are meant to do for the school were designed to help us speak and be heard through various means.

I thought about my book and the dream or, more accurately, the nightmare that my sister once had when the Virgin Mary visited her.

Chapter 2
TO WISH UPON THE VIRGIN MARY

Legend has it that if the Virgin Mary appears in your dream, she will make whatever you ask of her come true. One night, when my sister Niran was twelve years old, the Virgin Mary appeared in her dreams. The Virgin, wearing a bright blue robe, happily fluttered in front of Niran, like a butterfly over a sunflower. This was my sister's chance to cast her wish. She knew exactly what to wish for – that the Virgin save the house my father was building for his family. Each day, Niran had heard our parents talk and cry about how they were on the brink of losing it.

The Virgin Mary waited. Niran tried to part her lips and say, "Our house – " but she couldn't. Her voice choked. Soon the Virgin began to leave. Niran tried to crawl to the Virgin, but she could not reach her. The Virgin Mary moved farther and farther away until, like a bird flying into the sky, she blended with the air.

Niran opened her eyes, devastated that she had lost the opportunity to help save the house in Al Sikek.

Hay Al Sikek translates to the Railway Neighborhood. It is part of Al Karkh district, and it's located behind Baghdad Central Railway Station. Built by the British in 1953, the Baghdad Central Railway Station is the main train station, and the largest, in Baghdad, and it links the rail network to the south and north of Iraq. The station, once considered the "Jewel of Baghdad" for daily travelers, offered telegraph services. It had a bank, a post office, a saloon, shopping areas, a restaurant, and an office with printing presses that printed train tickets.

During the 1960s, my father worked for the railway station as the head of the bookkeeping department. The government gave him a house to rent for one dinar a month, which translates to living for free. Back then, prominent family men like engineers, doctors, and pilots lived in the district of Al Sikek. Each street had a security guard at the entrance. Our house had beautiful front and back yards with flowers tended by our gardener. Nearby stood a movie theater and a private club where my siblings went to hang out and swim.

The heavenly lifestyle became more heavenly in 1968 when Ahmad Hassan Al Bakr became president of Iraq. He gave all government employees free land in the district of Al Sikek, on which they could build homes. He allowed them to borrow money and required they pay it back little by little, through small deductions from their monthly salary. No one could pass up this deal.

My father built a big two-story house on his share of free land. At that time, our family consisted of eleven children: seven girls and four boys. My oldest two sisters were married to brothers. My father decided we would live on the first floor, and my married sisters and their families would live on the second floor. In the Middle East, homes are built from real brick and concrete, so they can last a lifetime. Unlike wooden houses, Middle Eastern homes do not need a new roofing every fifteen years. Married children, usually the sons, would build a second home on top of the first one. Then if yet another one married and decided to live at the same house, another house would be added atop the last. It was like making a cake, layer by layer.

My father loved his children dearly and wanted his married daughters to live near him. But my oldest brother warned him, "You might not have enough for the second story. Build the first one now, and if you have enough money left over, build the rest."

My father did not listen to my brother because one of his sons-in-law promised that he would help finish the house, *if need be*. My father pushed on. The house was completed. It stood on its feet with all its body parts. Missing were the interior necessities, such as the plumbing and electricity, painting, and floor tile. But money ran out. My father needed one thousand dinars, which was chump change at that time, though not to my father, who had already overused his money and resources. The son-in-law who promised he would help finish the house, *if need be*, relinquished his promise as easily as one passes gas. My father then went to his siblings to borrow the money. When they showed hesitation, he offered to do anything, even put the house in the borrower's names, for the one thousand dinars.

One thousand dinars would not have affected anyone's pockets, but it would have secured the lives of our entire household, including my married sisters and their families. In Iraq, once you bought a house, you owned it for life. Mortgages did not exist. It would have been so easy to lend that money, but one miserly aunt convinced the rest of the family members to turn down my father's request. She blamed his financial problems on his bad business tactics and his association with scoundrels. She strongly felt that he did not deserve any financial help, that even if he was given the one thousand dinars, he could not be trusted to execute the deal. Some wonder if she simply could not see our family prosper.

One greedy man of high position at my father's workplace

had his eye on our house that was one thousand dinars shy of completion. He told my father, "We gave you the land, lent you the money to build the house, and it is still not finished. You have to give it back to the government."

My father, an outspoken man, cursed him. This caused a feud. The man turned off the water and electricity on the rental house we lived in, forcing my mother to carry water back and forth from the neighbors. My siblings, who had exams during this time and could not study in the dark, spent the nights at my cousin's house.

Having missed the opportunity to request of the Virgin Mary to save the house, Niran decided to turn her rescue efforts elsewhere. She would ask for help from her friend and classmate Hayfa, the daughter of Iraq's president. Hayfa and Niran shared a desk at school. The teacher was not responsible for this particular seating arrangement. Hayfa registered in elementary school long after school started. When she entered her classroom, she spotted the one person who was not geeked by the presence of the president's daughter, my sister Niran, who was not only nonchalant but also a beautiful girl with full lips and big, fish-shaped eyes. She went up to Niran and asked her, "Can I sit beside you?"

"Fatima sits here," Niran said. "She's out of school because she's sick."

"When she returns, I will give her back her seat."

Hayfa and Niran quickly became friends. Hayfa had other sisters in different classrooms and like her, they were well-behaved and mingled casually with the rest of the schoolmates. A car drove Hayfa to school every morning and picked her up at the end of the day. She would come in with a headscarf that she quickly removed when she entered the classroom. Hayfa was older than the other students in the class, and she barely had any previous education. When the teacher asked her to go and write her name on the board, she wrote it so big that it nearly covered the entire board. She had no training in handwriting.

A pretty and generous girl, Hayfa brought lunch to school every day and had an allowance high enough to buy cake and a Pepsi. She always offered my sister the first sip of her Pepsi bottle. My sister would politely decline, saying, "You bought it, so you must have the first sip."

They went back and forth like that, but Hayfa always won. She had my sister take the first sip even if it meant waiting until recess was over and carrying on like this in class. Being the president's daughter, she would continue drinking her Pepsi inside the classroom, which was not permissible, because the teacher never reprimanded her.

Hayfa was a chatterbox. Every day in class she would tell my sister whatever happened inside her home the day before, who visited them, and who did not. Even while the teacher gave a lecture, she talked and talked. She stopped at nothing. One day, the teacher, unable to direct a message to Hayfa, called out my sister. "Please Niran, keep quiet because your talking is disrupting the classroom," she said.

"No, Miss, she was not the one talking," Hayfa responded. "I was."

Hayfa liked my sister very much, to where when Fatima, who previously shared my sister's desk, returned to class and wanted her seat back, Hayfa refused to give it up. Another time the teacher moved Niran to a different desk while Hayfa was absent. When Hayfa returned and saw what had happened, she told the teacher, "I want to sit next to Niran."

The teacher had to oblige.

Niran figured if she told Hayfa her troubles at home, her father, the president, could surely help out. Not only was he the president, but a neighbor. He lived only a few blocks from our house, and his uncle lived even closer. She was at first too shy to approach her, but over time, when the government cut off the electricity and water, leaving my mother in a heap of a mess, she finally had the courage to speak.

"My dear, I never even see my father," Hayfa said to my sister after listening to her. "When he comes home, I'm already asleep."

My sister missed an opportunity to ask the Virgin Mary for help, and being the friend of the president's daughter did her no good. Our family lost the house and moved out of the rental home and into a bad neighborhood where the kids on the block, for no known reason, threw stones against our windows. My father considered his options. He and his brother discussed selling their shares of the land in the then Christian village of Telkaif in northern Iraq. Their father had left them that land.

My father said to his family, "Since you did not lend me a thousand dinars to finish the house, at least give me the deeds to sell my share."

They agreed. The deeds were housed by the same miserly aunt who convinced the rest not to lend my father money. My father sent one of my older sisters to pick up the deeds. Each time my sister went there, this miserly aunt found an excuse not to give her the deeds. She said she could not find them, that she had misplaced them and had to dig for them. Five times my sister would take two buses to get to my aunt's house, and she would return empty handed. My father then went to get the deeds himself, and he received the same message. "Oh, I can't seem to find them. I seem to have misplaced them."

We lost the house my father had built. We were kicked out of the house we lived in. Then the man who feuded with my father ended up transferring him to the city of Samawah, located 174 miles southeast of Baghdad. As a result, my father worked all week and came home only during the weekend. This broke his spirit. By the time we left Iraq, we had little to our name. We certainly did not have the deeds. Years later, my aunt gave them to the other brother. Then Saddam announced that whoever had a rental in Al Sikek could consider themselves the owners of that house, for free. We'd missed yet another opportunity for prosperity. For decades to come, that became our family's pattern. How does one break such a pattern?

Chapter 3
MEETING MY NEW MENTOR

I eagerly waited for Wednesday night to arrive, for my scheduled call with my second-year mentor, Fiona. In preparation, I cleaned our three-bedroom home and even organized parts of the basement. Cicily, the woman I met at the writers retreat the year before, called early that morning. She said, "I'm on my way to Target, so I'm going to put you on speaker. I want to talk to you about your book. I'd like to represent you once you're done with it. I met with some of the editors from the retreat the other day and we talked about your work, how important it is, and how much you'd progressed from your first visit to the retreat to the second visit. You're one of the ones who will make it."

Not a shred of joy entered my heart. I heard this all before from my previous New York agent and editors: "You're a good writer! You write important stories! You will succeed!" Pass the sunflower seeds, please, and spare me the compliments. Nowadays, fancy words of encouragement mattered less to me than Big Boy's strawberry Belgium waffle with extra whip cream and ice cream topping. I longed for that hot golden, sometimes crispy, waffle with fresh strawberries, the juice trickling over the plate like a bride's long veil…

"I want you to send me the manuscript once it's finished," she said, interrupting my imaginary rendezvous with the Belgium waffle.

I consented, feeling no depth of truth to my consent. For three years, I had itched to write the "The End," but I couldn't. The manuscript needed a load of work, and forcing it into completion felt as unnatural and unhealthy as forcing a five-week embryo, which is the size of a grain of rice, into a fully developed baby.

We talked about the kids, work, and how she had wrecked her Saturn and went and bought a car. I listened, poured myself another cup of blueberry coffee, and put away the dishes. I froze when she announced that one of the writers at the retreat had recently finished her book. Dripping with envy, the benign not malicious type, my mind scrambled in different directions as I tried to understand, how could this be? Despite not having made a New Year's resolution, I did pack up my laptop the first morning of January and head to the coffee shop, determined to finish the book this year. I stopped taking freelance jobs and going to those good-for-nothing meetings with Iraqi-American businessmen. So how, despite all the time and effort I stuffed into my manuscript, was I nowhere near done? And in all truthfulness, the manuscript reeked of too many literary flaws.

"I need to stop going over the material I've already written and just finish the first draft," I said, changing my three-year-old son from his pajamas.

"That would be my advice," she said. "Once you finish the first draft, you'll have a better idea of what changes you need to make. Then you can go back and revise. And I'd be happy to look at it and make suggestions."

After we hung up, I dropped off my son to nursery school and then drove to Panera Bread to write. My schedule routine was as follows: wake up at 7:30 am; dress my daughter and send her off to school with her father; sit behind the computer and write from 8:30 am to whenever my son woke up, normally at around 10:30am or later; feed him; and, two days a week, prepare him for nursery school. Then I make the beds and tidy the house, and if I have not already done so the night before or we do not have enough leftovers, I prepare lunch. I drop off my son at school at noon, drive to the nearby Panera Bread, and spend two and a half hours writing and enjoying a coffee and bagel with cream cheese. I normally wrote an average of four-and-a-half hours per day, not counting any of the research, unless I ended up taking the kids to the library, which added another two hours.

I ordered my usual coffee, a toasted Asiago cheese bagel, and chive and onion cream cheese. Carrying my tray to the table, I received a call from one of my brother's wives. She said, "Where have you been, Weam? I haven't heard from you in a long time."

"I've been on a hiatus," I said happily as I set my tray on the table. "I'm on the verge of completing my book."

"What book?"

"The book I've been working on for almost three years."

She laughed. "Wouldn't it have been better if you'd spent those years getting a PhD and then you could have been a professor and made good money?"

I explained that the profession of writing, although it made little money, allowed me to stay home and raise my children. I love what I do, I said, and when the economy is down, as it is right now, doing what you love creates a very good life. She agreed, but my mood was still spoiled. As I tried to refocus on the task at hand, at writing, I wondered why my family constantly tried to change me into their version of me. This reminded me of my decision at the beginning of the year to stop answering calls from family and friends during my writing hours.

Later in the day, I took the kids to the library.

"Twenty-four dollars!" someone bellowed. "You've got to be kidding me!"

I woke up to the voice of a man arguing with the librarian at the checkout counter. I had come here to write, but after staring blankly at the computer screen for too long, I had rested my head on the table for a snooze.

"I could buy a car for that much!" he said.

I looked up and saw a man who appeared to be in his fifties dressed in black pants and a black leather jacket, a briefcase beside his legs.

"You guys are worse than the police!" he continued, so loud that his voice echoed in the library. "I'm never going to come in here again! I'm never going to read a book again! I didn't even read this book! I read one page and it was the worst page I ever read!"

He paused for a second as the librarian said something I could not comprehend, to which he responded, "You guys are worse than the police! You know how much the government owes me? They owe me hundreds of dollars! I'm an honest guy here! I came in and told you about the book being damaged when I could have just thrown it in the drop box and drove away and you couldn't have done a single thing about it…"

"Well, we have you here on record, sir," the librarian said.

"You still should appreciate me coming in to tell you this book accidently got damaged, and you're asking for twenty-four dollars! That's more than the cost of food I eat per month! Listen, I'm on welfare, and what kind of government place is this? You're worse than the police!"

Unable to suppress my laughter any longer, I allowed it to

burst into the air in the quietest way possible. As I watched the man walk out, I desperately wished to stop him, ask him to sit with me over coffee (I'd pay), and to tell me more about this late fee dilemma. It would have made for such an interesting conversation. But he left, and for the life of me, I could not stop laughing. Then I heard a woman ask her father, a white haired man with a cane, "Dad, do you want to watch *Sophie's Choice?*"

"It's kind of depressing," he said. "You kind of want to shoot yourself in the end."

"Yeah, that's true."

"Do they have dirty movies here?"

"No. No, they don't, Dad."

This triggered more laughter, and then I heard someone say, "You can't judge a poop by its cover," and I continued to laugh, a laughter which lasted throughout the drive home and during my time cleaning and preparing dinner for my husband. As I chopped onions, my children insisted I tell them what was so funny and I spluttered, between my laughing fits, "I can't explain it. You guys are too young to understand."

My laughter made me want to fold my seriousness into a laundry basket, place the basket in one of the astronaut shuttles scheduled to launch soon, and send it off into the universe. Ingvild Saelid Gilhus, a professor at the University of Bergen in Norway, wrote *Laughing Gods, Weeping Virgins: Laughter in the History of Religion*. In it, she talks about how the myth of laughter of derision and laughter of regeneration flourished in Mesopotamia, but the older version of it comes from Tel Al-Amarna in Egypt. Powerful deities in Akkadian and Hurrian mythologies used these forms of humor to maintain hierarchical order in Mesopotamia and to suppress ambition. She writes, on page 31, "In Mesopotamia, Israel, and Greece, humankind tried to attain a carefree existence and/or immorality, but was denied both. The relationship between humankind and gods, as Hesiod describes it, was antagonistic."

My mother always shot us scornful looks when we burst into laughter as a warning for us to stop such foolishness. She would say, "Don't laugh!" as though we were breaking the code of the Nasal Academy by cleaning our nostrils in public. She associated it with negativity, as evidently so did the older generation, who always posed for a picture with a serious, pensive, or even sad expression.

I wondered if our forefathers had not only oppressed our voices but also our innocent laughter in order to maintain the largest possible gap between the titles they granted themselves, gods, and the titles they granted ordinary people, men. But research has shown that suppressing or avoiding your emotions, which causes high anxiety and depression, in fact can make these emotions stronger.

I cracked three *noomi basra*, black dried whole limes, with my teeth to allow the citrus to flee from its confinement. These dried lemons, the size of golf-balls, add a sour, slightly bitter, and somewhat smoky taste to stews and soups. They are essential ingredients in Iran, Iraq, and the Gulf States and occasionally are used in northern Indian dishes. Transforming them from juicy limes to *noomi basra* requires first boiling the limes for a short time in saltwater and then laying them out in the sun to dry for several weeks, until their skin turns hard and their color becomes dark brown or black.

Together with chopped onions and two cans of chick peas, I threw the dried limes into the pot of chicken soup, known in Iraq as *tashreeb* and made with chicken, beef, or lamb. I allowed the dancing steam to bathe my face and the sound of the bubbling broth to soothe my ears as I gave thanks to the Creator. Then I warned my kids, "I'm going to make an important phone call now, and I don't want anyone to bother me, understand?"

They nodded with big, naughty smiles. I escaped into the bedroom, leaving the door wide open so I could hear any mischief, and I dialed Fiona's number. Sitting Indian-style on my bed, a pen and notebook in my lap, I listened to the phone rings.

"Hello," a woman answered.

"Hi, Fiona. This is Weam."

"Hello, Weam! It's wonderful to meet you!"

A door opened with the sound of her voice. The mystery of this year would soon start to unravel, bringing forth the areas I still needed to work on in order to bring my dreams to light. These thoughts relaxed me as we chit-chatted. I asked her to tell me a little about herself and how she ended up in Lynn's school.

"I'm originally from Canada, and then I moved to Arizona," she said. "My day job is a cancer clinic nurse. I have three beautiful kids. I'm Rainbow Energy, but I also balance with Nurturing Energy. I used this with my family, involving my kids in my housework, doing laundry while they read – things like that. I stumbled upon Lynn's work in 2002, through her books. I was suffering from a depression disorder and was travelling from cold weather, in Canada, to a warm climate. I wanted to read a book along the way and stopped at a bookstore and it was right there. I took a look at it, decided to pass it up, walked away, and saw it again right in front of me. It was like, 'What's this?'"

"That's sort of how I ended up in Lynn's school. I had gone with my niece into Barnes & Noble. Our children were with us, and she volunteered to watch them play at the Thomas the Train table while I browsed around. I had not had the luxury of browsing alone in a bookstore in a long time, and the first place I went to was the reference section to look at books about writing. I saw this book called *Writing Spirit* sitting oddly on the shelf. It was the only copy, and it was as if it did not belong there. The cover had a painting of large palms and the table of contents talked about power animals and shamanism and I could not make heads or tails of how this related to writing. I skimmed through it and found that I could not put it down. I did not want to buy it either, but yet that's what I did."

"Why didn't you want to buy it?" she asked.

"I was in a really bad place with my work," I said, sighing at the memory. "I did not love it anymore, and half the time I woke up in the morning wishing I would quit writing and find something else to do. The last thing I wanted was to read a book about writing, but that's exactly what I needed. I needed a book about writing that was different than any other book about writing I had ever read. I wasn't looking for a 'how to' book. I knew 'how to.' I had been writing for twenty years."

"Hmmm."

"When I read it, I remembered *why* I had become a writer in the first place. I remembered my calling. My love and passion for my writing started to resurface. At the back of the book, Lynn said we could schedule a session with her, so I did that. I was hoping she could give me some advice about my career. She recommended the Mystery School. I was hesitant at first. I did not want to fall for a gimmick. At the same time, I was willing to do anything to move my career forward, and something about her teachings had that ancient quality that my people have, but which they have forgotten to use."

"Who are your people?"

"The Christians of Iraq, the tribes of ancient Mesopotamia.

Our bloodline traces back to the land of the Chaldees, where Prophet Abraham was born and lived until God called him."

A deep silence seasoned our atmosphere. That silence, along with the incense, took me to the desert, where I could almost smell the sand and feel the hot sun.

"And where are you with your writing today?" she asked.

"I'm in a totally different place. I love my writing, and I am more committed to it than ever. Last year, I cleaned out quite a bit of toxicities from my life that were holding me back. I had no idea I was carrying such a load of negativities and addictions. I used to think that addictions only had to do with physical factors like tobacco, drugs, alcohol, food, sex, television. I found out that there are much subtler addictions, like being addicted to drama, worry, comparing, complaining."

"Lynn has said that the worst kinds of addictions are addictions to emotions, like fear or sadness, for example. She says that they keep us in a kind of drugged sleep and that it's very important, although difficult, to break out of their cycle."

"The best part about the changes is how they influenced my family. My relationship with my husband and children is so much better. I even remodeled my home last year, and in doing so, created the perfect space for me, as a wife and mother and as a writer."

"These are great accomplishments within a year's time."

"Yes, I realize that, and I'm grateful for it. Yet I still have not finished the book I'm working on. I have the story, I have the years of experience – I wrote three books in my twenties – and yet I keep getting stuck. The running around I do and the feeling of never being caught up causes me to beat myself up. Today was so bad that my head hurt."

"I want you to scan what you just told me and tell me what

you see."

"I see chaos. I'm scattered."

"You're leaking your energy and scattering it again."

Why did she say *again*? How did she know that was what I did before?

"That's why you'll love this year," she said. "This year you are going to become strong and hold your energy and stand in sacred witness. All that chaos will disappear, and your head won't hurt. You will review your journal in December and by then, you will find that you are holding the energy and not dropping it."

I imagined women from the East who elegantly balance heavy and large items on their head, such as buckets of water, fruit or laundry, and bundles of firewood. With a strong neck, good posture, and with relative ease, they travel on foot for miles, their muscles having been trained and strengthened for this task since childhood. But heavy bulks are physical objects that can be seen, touched, and measured. How does one hold energy, something that, in a sense, cannot be defined?

I did not ask that question. Instead, I told her about how my journey last year helped individualize me from my extended family while maintaining my love for them. I added, "I do feel that I have to keep some distance to protect the road I'm on."

"You will find that will change one day."

The certainty in which she said those words changed the picture I was holding up about my family. The grudges I had toward them suddenly melted away, as if zapped by a sunray, and my memory dove into the ocean of our history, a history which began long before our births. I swam like a mermaid through our eternal love, my lungs filled with joy at the idea that possibly this year our relationship together would be reborn into a more magnificent experience.

I shared my feelings with Fiona, and she said, "If you are thinking in the shape of the wheel, the last part is east, where you figured out the bigger picture to all of this. East is the Wise One. Being upset is west, emotional. It is the teenager not getting what they want. The north is Spirit, the part where you become still and allow space in your consciousness for thoughts to come in. Unless you make space in your consciousness, nothing can change because the container is full."

The next day, when my husband came home from work, he handed me a gift bag with a bottle of perfume inside of it. "Happy Valentine's Day," he said.

He also placed the mail on the counter. On top was a letter from A Room of Her Own Foundation (AROHO). My heart stopped for a moment. Just prior to my eyes falling on the envelope, I thought how having my own money could give me the financial freedom I needed, the help I was looking for. AROHO is a nonprofit organization working on behalf of women writers. Through grants, awards, and other types of support, they help advance Virginia Woolf's belief that "women need money and a room of their own if they are to write." I had submitted an application last year for its $50,000 Gift of Freedom Award.

I stared at the letter, afraid to open it. My mind moved around the miniature garden of dreams I had planted over the years which had difficulty growing for lack of financial water. For several minutes I allowed myself to experience being lifted from the bottom of the sea by a large amount of money brought from the Pleiades, the rainbows, or wherever else.

I left the letter on the dresser and continued to clean. I finished washing the dishes and placed my husband's dinner on the table before I slipped into the bedroom again, and leaning against the dresser, I tore open the envelope. The miniature garden of dreams drifted away at the sight of the first few lines, like a lost sailboat in the hopes of being rescued pushed further into the ocean by a strong gush of wind. I folded the letter and wept. All the hours I'd spent writing the long winded and complicated grant proposal! I would have been better off working on the book! I've had it – with the book, with money, with rejections, with doing everything on my own! I've had it!

My husband and son walked in. I fumbled for the Kleenex but not in time to cover my tears. My husband asked, "Why are you crying?"

I wished to hide under the bed. I didn't want anyone to see my failure, a failure which kept following me like a ghost. He continued to stand there, expecting an answer when all I wanted to do was drop on the bed and cry, alone.

"It's nothing," I said.

He became upset as his jealousy rekindled. When we first got married, my husband felt left out by my inner world which, he thought, was crowded with my love for writing, spirituality, and past experiences. He stormed out of the room, my son behind him, and I heard his mumbles down the hallway, which caused my crying to intensify. I loved my husband's masculinity, his expectation that women should be real women and men should be real men. I admired his dark and good looks and his wild behavior, along with his enthusiasm and generosity. But he did not deal with his feelings in a thoughtful, intelligent way. He often presumed he knew what *my* feelings, thoughts, and fears were even after I tried to explain that his interpretations were entirely inaccurate. He was a fire sign who I often wished to calm down by throwing ice cubes down his shirt.

My son returned into the room, insisting I let him eat Combos and drink milk at his computer desk rather than the kitchen table. "No!" I said angrily, my hand grazing over his cheeks.

Even though it was not a slap, my fingernails had barely touched his cheek, he cried, "You hoot my feelings!"

I felt horrible, not about the rejection anymore but about what was a hundred times dearer to me – my family, my priority. I was tired of taking my writing so seriously that it was playing with my emotions. I had to put myself in check and return to enjoying a loving time with my husband, children, mother, and siblings. The last words Fiona had said last night before we hung up was that this year was going to be fun. The word "fun" had buzzed in my head all day, like a craving.

My son and I made up, and during bedtime, he cuddled beside me. I apologized to him again for snapping at him, and he again said, "It's awight, Momma." I grabbed Lynn Andrew's *Star Woman*, a required reading, from over my nightstand and read a passage where Agnes, Lynn's teacher, says the following words to her:

> Now doesn't exist, because you don't completely accept who you are right now. You think you will accept yourself when Twin Dreamers returns or when you become better recognized or a better shamaness. But none of this is true. Nothing is ever enough if you don't accept yourself right this moment as complete. If you don't, there will always be a sense of longing, and you will die with that longing even if you are a famous writer, or invincible as a healer.

Allowing these words to sink deep into my spirit, I closed the book, hugged my son, and fell asleep.

Chapter 4
SLIPPING INTO YOUTH

"**I** will see my hands in my dreams!" I said to myself as I lay in bed at night, gazing softly and easily at my hands, as instructed by my study guide. I looked at my hands, front and back, as if I'd never seen them before and set my intent that I'll be able to see them in my dreams. Every night, my dreams were visited by various sounds, images, tales, and sensations, but not my hands. Lynn said not to give up on this task, as it required a lot of practice. I continued to try and find my hands in my dreams, but to no avail.

One day I dreamt that I was sitting between two of my sisters in a rug shop, in an Arabic country heavy in Islamic culture. The majority of people there were men with traditional Arabic clothing. The women wore veils but not ones that completely covered their faces. Bonnie, a woman I detached myself from last year, sat beside me. She was trying to raise funds for my film. I thought, "Oh no, not again." I ignored her and attempted to have a conversation with the natives.

Suddenly I saw my mother in front of me, sitting on a special chair. She was not wearing her dentures, and she looked incredibly wise. She began to tell a story of the day I was born, how she could tell I would end up doing great things. My sisters and I hushed each other as we tried to listen to what she had to say. Then she said, "I knew you were going to become something great from the way which you uttered 'duh' when you came out."

I woke up, confused about the meaning of the dream. Was my mother making fun of me or was she genuinely giving me credit for something? I couldn't tell. For the most part, I was a dutiful daughter with wild days few and far between. I did what I was told, no questions asked, but sometimes, I could not do it properly.

One morning, when I was a child still living in Baghdad, my mother sent me to buy fresh bread from the bakery. It was a Friday, the Muslim day of rest, when my family ate a hearty breakfast together. Since we did not have a kitchen table big enough to seat a dozen people, we spread blankets and bed sheets on the floor and placed the food in the center – dishes of fried beef with tomatoes, various egg omelets, hot mint tea, and fresh hot *samoon*, diamond-shaped pocket bread.

Dressed in my nightgown, I entered the bakery. Surrounded by its warmth and delightful aroma, I made it to the brick oven, weaving through the crowd of men and women in black robes and children waving dinars. Customers could see the rising bread through the small flaming oven window. The baker dropped the hot bread into a nearby tub with a large wooden spatula, and customers quickly grabbed it. The process repeated itself many times as I stood there, awaiting my turn. Standing at the edge of the tub, I was the nearest one to the bread, but before I could reach for it, other hands scooped it up at a speed I could not match. I did not interrupt their great haste, not through words or action, as I continued to wait my turn.

My father or brother, I can't remember which, showed up before my turn came. The family had grown worried over my long absence and came to fetch me. Neither they, nor I, understood why I had failed to catch any fish although the fish was at my fingertips. It might have been that incident that began my mother's habit of telling me, far into my adulthood, "Don't be shy! Speak up!"

But in this dream where we sat in the rug shop, she was probably saying, "Lighten up." Yes, Mother, now I can lighten up. I finally finished the first draft of the manuscript and felt relief, even though I knew I had much more work ahead of me. The manuscript had many problems. It was missing a style and rhythm, a depth that required a literary, not journalistic, voice. It looked like a Christmas tree without the ornaments or lights.

However, nothing could inspire me to revise at this time, so I decided to abandon this literary forest and run outside into the city, to celebrate with family at an Arabic nightclub, to have fun. I told Fiona all about it, adding, "The funny thing was that, even though there were obstacles to going, and it almost wasn't going to happen…"

"Why was it not going to happen?" she asked. "Were you sabotaging it?"

"No, I felt I was being tested. Someone said, 'Oh, the weather is bad. It's snowing. The roads will be slippery.' There were issues with babysitters, who's going to be the designated driver, etc., but I held firm and said, 'I want to go.'"

"You allowed yourself to stay centered, and you didn't let the obstacles happen."

I relived that night – sipping wine while listening to Arabic music, smoking a hookah, and watching women pour their hearts and souls out through the movements of their waists and hips. During the Iraqi songs, women with long hair that fell sensually around them like a scarf performed the *kawleeya*, a dance where they swing their hair in circles and whip it back and forth. They glided their head from side-to-side in a delicate and sassy shimmy-like movement.

I find *kawleeya* to be the most artful of the Arabic dances, despite the term being derogatory. Kawleeya relates to gypsies who dance and do sexual favors for money. It's the name of a village about a hundred miles southeast of Baghdad, a territory where Romani people emigrated to from South Asia, particularly from India. They separated into two groups, one traveling northward and becoming the Romani-speaking European Gypsies. The other traveled to the Middle East and spoke the Domari language. In Iraq, they isolated themselves from the rest of the country. After the collapse of Saddam's regime, fanatic Muslim groups attacked this village, killing many and forcing the rest to flee.

At the nightclub, the band member with the doumbek drum caught my attention. He held this musical instrument, which is what the belly dancer danced to, under his arm and placed it sideways on his lap as he sat. The doumbek is a hand drum with a goblet shape used mostly in the Middle East, North Africa, and Eastern Europe. It creates the beats for the belly dancer. The original use of goblet drums in Babylonia and Sumeria dates from as early as 1100 BCE. Traditional drum heads were animal skin, commonly goat and also fish. Modern drums usually use synthetic materials for drum heads, including fiberglass and aluminum.

I found the drum for me, I thought. One of the school assignments was to choose a personal drum to pray with, whether with our family, with people who come to us, or just to contemplate. My friend, who I call in my books the Red Indian, once told me that before they make their drums, some people talk to the tree to give up their pieces for making things like drums and pipes. By talking to the trees, one makes the wood become alive. He said, "We make our drums out of cedar and make thirteen sides, and you stretch it with elk or deer hide."

"What do the thirteen sides represent?" I asked.

"It represents thirteen moons of the year. We have thirteen seasons because we work with the moon. Females also have thirteen cycles in the year. This is how we do things in the Great Lakes. Other tribes do things differently. We don't fight about how you do something. Everyone washes their faces, but everyone does it differently. Whatever you learn is great, but you have to remember there are a lot of different ways to do things. Like in your area, the end result is they want peace and prosperity from the Creator, and they do that by enjoying what they do." He paused and then added, "So anyway, if you talk to cedar tree when you make it, you have a live drum. I had a drum, but I gave it away to a young man."

"Why did you give your drum away?"

"I was interested in him doing well. He just graduated high school and couldn't find his way so I gave him my drum so he would not go partying and smoke weed."

There was a full moon on Oscar Sunday. I meditated, giving away my critical grudging self. Meditating serves not only the meditator but, step-by-step, it moves the energy of divine light, love, and power throughout one's family, community, and the earth. Additional benefits surface when this practice is done during the full moon period. A full moon signifies completion and is an ideal time for letting go of things that no longer serve you, although the Red Indian has a different definition of it. I once asked him, "What's the difference between new moon and full moon?"

"They're the same thing," he said. "They're both full. It's just that you have to see the new moon in the daytime because it's full. You can't see it at night because it's on the other side of the earth. You see the full moon at night. The moons were used to decide the best time to plant something. On full moon, you plant things in the ground, like potatoes, because the seeds do better. On the new moon, you plant things above the ground, like cherries. Much is controlled by the moon, like fishing, hunting, planting, and the seasons. I say controlled because you cannot do it, but it has an effect on everything, including animals, especially wild animals.

"Because of religion and how people are taught, it has different effects on different people. On full moon night, the police say they're busy and they have a hard time dealing with people. People are drinking and there's a lot of crime. It's not because that's the natural way of responding, but they've been taught that way. There are a thousand things that people are raised on that make them behave poorly. In countries other than the United States the effect is not as bad. If you go in the Pacific Rim Islands, if they have not been taught about monsters and goblins when they were little, then they can be very relaxed and enjoy the full moon as a gift from God and not, 'Oh, I have to behave like an asshole because it's a full moon.'"

Ben Affleck won best picture for *Argo*. He thanked a zillion people and credited his success to working hard, etc. – all the stuff that most people talk about – but he also added, "I learned I can't hold a grudge."

His words held up a mirror for me. My heart had been soaked in grudges for too long, like someone had dumped a tub of syrup on top of it and allowed it to languish there until it turned hard and became difficult to chew. My relationship with my siblings, despite the great time we had at the night club, refused to return. I could not tear down the wall I'd built between us.

"I'm not sure whether I'm ready to tear down the wall yet," I told Fiona during our next conversation.

"I know that you'll know when the time is right," she said. Then she asked me how I was doing with the assignments. "Have you observed nature in respect to you and have you read the barometer?"

"I have not read the barometer. As for observing nature, I don't really understand what I'm looking for when I listen to the wind or the chirping of a bird."

"When you suddenly look at the trees and see the wind blowing, if your attention is coming from the east, you ask yourself, 'What was I just thinking? What was I doing?' Notice that and take note. Did you have a problem and an answer came to you? Same with animal sounds. Pose a question. If it's always the crow showing up, what's the crow saying? Did you get the message? When you do get the message, he will then leave, unless he's your power animal. In this way, your confidence will build, and you will see your answers are there. All you have to do is go out there and explore. What do kids like to do? Explore." After a pause, she asked, "Is this making sense, or is it scaring you?"

"It's not scaring me. I really enjoy this."

"You are very open and receptive, because you're not interrupting with but, but, but."

"The other day, something happened that switched my point of view. It was Saturday morning, and I noticed I couldn't write. I gravitated toward the couch, and with my kids beside me, read one of Lynn's books. There was a section where Lynn complains that she feels she's never doing enough, and her teachers remind her that she works very, very hard. I felt as if they were speaking to me. Right there and then, I allowed myself to take a nap."

"A lot of the overdoing and such is the way you leak energy, spreading yourself out too thin," she said. "You already noticed, picked up on what you needed to do, and took time to sleep. You would not have done that eight weeks ago. You would not have honored that. You're already changing your container, your being. You are healing that part of you that is hidden in your children. You are healing yourself."

Lynn and my mentors often compared our healings and transformation to the peeling of an onion. With each teaching, a new layer is peeled off until you get to the heart of your spirit. You peel and you practice and you fine-tune your abilities, feelings, and activities in the world of non-ordinary reality, over and over again until you achieve what she calls the *Fine Art of Mastery*. It may take a hundred years, but it's natural. A worker bee, for instance, will toil for an entire lifetime (approximately six weeks) to make about three drops of honey.

A silence followed as a topic thickened in my head, giving me mixed messages.

As I looked at my daughter's personalized photo magnet on the refrigerator, I considered whether to open another wound by telling Fiona about certain resentments I still had against my family. On one hand, this wound desperately wanted to express itself. On the other hand, it wanted to hide in the woods.

"I want to address something, but I don't want it to be a complaint," I said. "I just want to change a certain part of my story so it doesn't continue to repeat itself and I can move on."

I tried to explain, but Fiona could not understand where I

was coming from. To clarify, I gave her an example. The other day I had spoken to my cousin, who was married with children. She told me that when she worked on the weekends, her mother came and spent the night. Not only did her mother watch the kids, but she cooked and kept the house tidy. I couldn't help but feel hurt that despite my large family, who all lived within a mile or two, I often felt I had no one to turn to. Of my tribe, only two ever offered to help, one of whom was in no position to help, given her situation, which was too long a story to recite. So really, there was mostly one person and a few others for emergency backups.

"For a long time, I envied the women who didn't have a career, some not even a job, who had more help offered to them so that they could get to the mall and buy a new dress than I had been offered when I needed a breather once in a great while. What really hurts is that I've helped raise the majority of my thirty-plus nieces and nephews. I played a strong role in their lives before I got married, and to the best of my abilities, I still do, even if it's on a smaller scale."

"I want you to close your eyes and tell me where the pain is," Fiona said.

"It's in my heart."

"See yourself sitting with a blanket in front of your heart. Ask the pain what is its purpose?"

"I see the word strength."

"Ask it to be more specific."

"Issues of unworthiness."

"What else?"

"It keeps wanting to slip away."

"No, keep it there. Don't let it slip away. Ask if it's okay for it to step aside so you can see what's behind it?"

I did that and I was shocked to see me, in my early twenties, in one of my beautiful feminine summer outfits. I was holding bags of newly bought clothes. I looked, as I always did back then, bright enough to light a room.

"Can she see you?" asked Fiona.

"Yes," I replied, tears rolling down my face.

"Can you try to get her attention, to talk to her?"

"It's a little hard, to be honest."

"That's okay. Take your time."

"Looking at me, she is surprised – to see my lack of freedom."

"Okay, so she's shocked. Can she tell you what she needs to say to you? Why she has come back to you?"

I silenced myself in order to listen to her, or me.

"It has taken a lot of courage for you to call her here and for her to come here," said Fiona.

"Remember me."

"Remember me?"

"Yes, that's what she said. She wants me to remember her." I was sobbing by now. "She was such a carefree spirit. She had a big heart and few curfews and limitations, or so that's how she felt. And she was great with children. Sometimes, when I go off on my children, I remember her and think how she had never ever treated one of her nieces or nephews like that. She had a lot of patience with them."

"I want you to apologize to her for not allowing her to have the time and space to have fun and to promise her that from now on, you will let her have fun. Can you tell her that out loud?"

"Yes," and I told her.

After the younger me's shock at seeing what had become of me and my freedom, she quickly got over that, as she was good at not dwelling on anything or holding grudges. She grabbed my hands and took me from one store to the next, dolling me up.

"Now that you see how much fun it is to go shopping at the mall with her, you can call her to do that anytime you want," said Fiona. "Is there anything she wants to give you?"

"She gave me a hug."

"Whenever you're ready, say goodbye to her and let her go play in the mall. Tell her you'll be back because you, too, had fun. Just put a little sage down on your blanket and come back up."

"I wish I can keep her," I said, not wanting to come back.

"You do have her. I want you to meditate for five minutes every day with her and she'll start revealing things to you so you won't have to carry what you have to carry about your relatives. That's the beginning of healing. You already caught her and recognized her."

My tears continued to pour forth, extracting the pent-up emotions imprisoned in my soul. I didn't want to let her go. Her presence sweetened my nerves, and I remembered how magnificent and rare she really was: her pure heart, her bright attitude, her desire to help others, her wide dreams, her strong faith and belief in herself, her ability to allow others' ignorance to easily bounce off of her.

"I miss her," I said. "I want her to be a part of me once again."

"Now you change that statement of 'wanting that' because you just went there and brought a little bit of that person back. In bringing her back to you, she becomes you."

I could tell from my children's commotion that my husband had returned home from work. He walked into the room to change, saw me crying, and acted like it was no big deal. I laughed a hearty laugh.

"What's so funny?" Fiona asked.

"My husband just walked in, saw me crying, and left the room like okay, everything is normal. I think he's getting too used to this."

We cracked up, and then my daughter walked in crying uncontrollably. Still carried away by laughter, I didn't bother to ask her what was wrong, but she took the liberty to tell me. She had lent her doll's dress to her cousin, and now she had changed her mind and wanted it back. Feeling light and sleepy, I did nothing but listen to her cry. It did not bother me and neither did my son playing the iPod next to my ear with the volume full blast. Nothing mattered at that moment. I had found a powerful friend, and it was I.

Chapter 5
MY BRILLIANT CAREER

In my freshman year at Macomb Community College, I signed up for *Intro to Film* because I wanted to fit one or two easy classes into my otherwise heavy semester. The instructor for this class, which was held in the theater auditorium, had the interesting ability to memorize names. The first day of class, he went around asking each student their name. Then, with a proud smirk, he regurgitated the names without a mistake. I was impressed, until he declared that *Gone with the Wind* was the worst movie ever made.

An Arabic copy of *Gone with the Wind* was the first novel I ever read. I read it at nine years old, when my family and I lived in Amman, Jordan, awaiting our visas to come to America. Scarlett O'Hara and her people hooked me to the point where I had to be dragged to breakfast, lunch, and dinner. Intrigued by this southern belle, I could have happily skipped all meals and never went hungry. My siblings treated me to the movies after I finished reading the book, and I got to watch *Gone with the Wind* on the big screen with Arabic subtitles. It was the first time I had been in a movie theater.

Book or film, I idolized *Gone with the Wind*. And here was an instructor, a professional film critic, calling the movie the worst movie ever made. I waited to hear validation of his observation. I wanted to know how naïve I and many others were to think it so magnificent. What simpletons we were! Just falling for whatever the media and film critics said, although at nine years old, I had not heard any reviews of that film or any film. I did not know what reviews were. But that's it. I was nine years old! What did I know?

"I will not get into the multitude of reasons that *Gone with the Wind* is the worst film ever made," he said, unable to release his ongoing smirk. "That would take up the entire semester. But let me emphasize that this film was by far the worst film ever made."

I was confused, to say the least. At the Twelfth Academy Awards held in 1940, *Gone with the Wind* set a record for Academy Award wins and nominations. It was the first movie made entirely in color, so it became the first color film to win Best Picture. Why and how could this man call it the worst film ever made? It was absurd to destroy a good movie and not bother to explain *why*. As an instructor who taught *Intro to Film*, he must have a valid reason worthy of expression. But he did not have a reason, or if he did, he did not share it. Instead, he had us watch a movie he did value, *My Brilliant Career*.

The lights dimmed, and I was ready to put my feet over the empty seat in front of me and fall asleep. The first scene of the film was of a farm girl, Sybylla, pacing in her home, reading from a notebook. It was 1897, somewhere in Australia. "Dear fellow countrymen," she reads, "just a few lines to let you know that this story is going to be all about me. So in answer to many requests, here's the story of my career." She then reflects, sits down at her desk, and passionately writes, "Of my brilliant career! I make no apologies for being egotistical, because I am."

Her character captured my attention instantly, and I watched, with great intrigue, Sybylla continue to express herself on paper. "I have always known that I belonged to the world of the art, and the world of literature, and music, and the world of culture and elegance." As she writes, a sand storm whirls and sneaks its way through the open doors and windows of her house. Sybylla, entranced by her own writing, does not notice the incredible commotion outside. Her father and brother toil to gear the farm animals to safety. She ignores it all, even when her mother shouts out her name. She remains in her own little world.

I felt that the story of my life was about to appear before my eyes. It sort of did. A poor farm girl wants to be a writer. That desire creates a struggle against a powerful set of conventions. Most of the people around her want to marry and settle down. That is not what she wants – well, not until a handsome, kind, and wealthy man appears and sweeps her off her feet. Sybylla is tempted to leave her dreams behind to marry this man, but in the end, she chooses not to. She happily chooses her own way.

The instructor turned off the projector, turned on the lights, and walked up to the stage with a huge grin. "So, what did you think about Sybylla's final decision?"

"She lost the battle," said one of the male students.

The instructor laughed. "Yes, she lost the battle, but she won the war!"

During break, I went to the restroom, entered one of the stalls, and cried, cried to have discovered someone like me, someone who wanted a career and was willing to relinquish marriage to do it. I chose to follow her footsteps. I made that choice with full intent, and then I forgot I made it. Forgetting I'd made that choice caused struggles and contradictions whenever I was in relationships. It took almost fifteen years for me to rec-ognize the decision I had made. I had sent out a message to the universe that my career came first, and so whenever I was in a relationship it would naturally, eventually, falter.

When I saw the role I had played in my status as a single woman, I decided to switch it around. I did not have to do what Sybylla did. I was not her, living in the 1800s. I did not have to choose career over husband and children or vice versa. I could have both. How I could have both was the question I seemed unable to answer after I got married and had kids.

To avoid tension and conflict with my husband, I spent fewer days at the coffee shop. Warren Community Center provided a wonderful alternative. The Center had a fitness area, indoor waterpark, café, an auditorium, an outdoor park and private garden, and a daycare center where patrons could drop off their kids for up to two hours a day, for as little as $4.50 for two kids. This place helped me tremendously, and I found it interesting that I had forgotten it existed although a few years prior I had come across it and made a note to myself that when my children were older, I would use it.

Sometimes, to avoid the monotony of sitting behind the computer in an ultra-quiet setting where the sound of someone's phone ringing caused a lot of upheaval, we also went to Barnes & Noble. The kids ordered their pizza pretzels and drinks, I had my white chocolate mocha or caramel macchiato with nonfat milk, and we carried our food to the kids' section. I sat on the large wooden chair and situated the food on another empty chair, took out my journal, and began to write. My daughter would hang out on the stage and pretend she was a teacher. My son played at the Thomas the Train table. I wrote to my heart's content, and I would arrive home in time to make dinner for my husband, get the kids fed and ready for bed, and be on time for my weekly call with my mentor or a conference call with Lynn.

"It's finally sunny in Arizona," Lynn said when she got on the phone. "It was snowing here just a few weeks ago."

I pressed *6 to mute the conversation from my end. Lynn soon said a prayer and asked us to close our eyes and imagine ourselves in a place we love, that gives us wonderful inspiration. I took a moment to center myself and gave thanks, but I could not close my eyes as I was chopping cucumbers and garlic cloves for the cucumber and yogurt salad. Despite the noise - my husband sat on the couch, his iPad blasting Arabic music – I listened, did the dishes, and sorted today's mail before the moderator began with the first question. I grabbed a pen and notebook and headed into my room.

A caller from Germany asked why the second year is called *Face of the Earth Lodge*. Lynn explained that this was a tradition from South America. They called their altars *Face of the Earth* to honor Mother Earth as a life force, with Father Sky bringing his inspiration. She reminded us, as she often did, that life never ends, that life is a circle.

The moderator then read a question from a woman in Argentina who could not be on the call because she did not speak English. The Argentinian described her ability to see forms and beings, and when she saw them, they were like x-rays and nightlights.

"That's an incredible ability that should be perfected," said Lynn. "And we're all coming to that. Let me explain."

She told us the story of when she had given a lecture in the Temple of Hathor in Egypt. She and several others were asked to go into the tunnels underneath the sanctuary. These tunnels were pretty tight and there were perfect and extensive petroglyphs everywhere, hundreds and hundreds of them. Lynn wondered how they'd done this without an electric light. How did they see to make these extraordinary drawings?

"Then I realized, of course, someone knew how to use nightlight," she said. "They could see in the dark, and they could produce a kind of light that would allow them to do what they were doing because there was no way that a torch or something like that would continue to burn in that atmosphere."

I thought of my trip in Washington last year, when Leslie brought me to a past life experience where I saw a very young girl, a nun, in a large and dark sanctuary. The young girl was frightened, running from one corner to another. Leslie asked me if I knew what country I was in, but I did not know. She asked me which temple I was in. I did not know that either. She named off several temples, and when she said the Temple of Hathor, I said, "I think that's it."

By the time I returned my attention to the call, there was another question from the woman in Germany. She wanted to know how to handle listening to painful stories, like that of a friend who was terribly abused as a child. She realized that, whenever confronted with such stories, whether in person or through television, she tended to take flight. A part of her did not want to be there witnessing the pain.

"Of course not," said Lynn. "In a way, it's disturbing. However, if you can move yourself into a larger vision of understanding that people have asked – and this seems painful – but people have asked for the experiences they've come into for very good reasons. To make an aspect of yourself stronger you sometimes have to go through really difficult times, and if you can understand that and see how wonderful that is – that your friend survived it! Acknowledge that! Say to that person, 'Yes, I hear you, how difficult that must have been, but look at the magnificent person you are now. And look how much stronger that made you and how much more aware you are than most people could ever be who have not had that kind of abuse.' Do you see?"

"Yes, I can see that," said the caller.

"You never hold that pain because it's not your experience," Lynn said. "But you certainly can understand it. People who talk about their problems basically want to be heard. They want to know that someone cares enough to hear them. You can't solve their problem. You can't change what they went through. It does no good to pick up that energy and hold it. You feel it and you let it wash away. It is her life song. It is not yours."

These words helped me finally let go of a story that had haunted me since December, the shooting at Sandy Hook Elementary School in Newton, Connecticut. For over a month after the incident, I often imagined the faces of twenty innocent first graders whose last sight was that of a horrific perpetrator, and the six adults, also shot to death, who tried to protect them. The news anchor said that the children were left in the gym that night so the police could continue their investigation.

I'd cried when I imagined the empty beds, filled with their scents and stuffed animals, in their parents' homes. The shooting happened on a Friday, and had these children returned home that night, they would have had supper with their families, chatted about what happened in school, and asked questions about their weekend plans, as my first-grader did when she came home. I thought of their young siblings, suddenly confronted by a vacuum that would impact them for the rest of their lives.

The Monday after the Sandy Hook shooting, all the schools' doors were closed as tight as the doors of a plane flying in the air. The staff in the school office watched through the window for anyone who approached the front doors. If they recognized you, or you did not look like a killer, they slightly opened the door, you declared your purpose for being on school grounds – "I want to drop off my daughter's lunch" or "I'm a little late for my son's nursery class" – you did your thing, and then you went on your way. This procedure went on until a buzzing system with video cameras was installed in the school so that the office ladies did not have to go back and forth and back and forth to ID people at the door.

Not a day went by that I dropped off my children at school without the memory of Sandy Hook and without feeling sad over how many bolts we had to use to keep ourselves and loved ones safe. The excitement I once had about sending my children off to school was snatched away, replaced by images of suicide bombers who haunted this earth more and more each day. The list of school-related attacks in the United States is long, in the hundreds. The oldest recorded one took place at Enoch Brown School, during the Pontiac War.

On July 26, 1764, four Lenape American Indian warriors entered a log schoolhouse of white settlers in what is now Franklin County, Pennsylvania. Inside were the schoolmaster, Enoch Brown, and twelve young students. Brown pleaded with the men to spare the children before being shot and scalped. The men then began to tomahawk and scalp the children, killing eleven of them. One boy who had been scalped survived. Reports claim that when the three Indians returned to their village and showed the scalps, their elder chief rebuked them as cowards for attacking children.

I asked the Red Indian about this type of violence, and he said, "We never warred with the Europeans, but there were several Native groups who retaliated because their families were killed."

Just a few weeks before the Enoch Brown incident, Governor John Penn formally announced the promise of bounties to be paid to the white man for Indian scalps. And the year prior, a white gang, the Paxton Boys, murdered six Indians, then a few days later, killed fourteen members of a peaceful Indian settlement that for more than seventy years had lived at Conestoga near Lancaster. The Indians fought back by killing and scalping anyone across the colony of Pennsylvania, disregarding age, gender, or condition.

Lenape families were matrilocal; newlywed couples would live with the bride's family, where her mother and sisters could also assist her with her growing family. Children belonged to their mother's clan, from which they gained social status and identity. The mother's eldest brother was more significant as a mentor to the male children than was their father, who was of another clan. Hereditary leadership passed through the maternal line, and women elders would remove leaders of whom they disapproved. Agricultural land was managed by women and allotted according to the subsistence needs of their extended families. Most Lenape were pushed out of their homeland by expanding European colonies during the eighteenth century after losses from intertribal conflicts. Their communities were weakened by newly introduced diseases, mainly smallpox, and violence perpetuated by Europeans.

"Whatever you're reading is their story," said the Red Indian. "It's what they [the Europeans] wrote. You have to look at who wrote the story, and usually there are five reasons why the story happened. A lot of reasons why Natives retaliated were because they had no reason to be there anymore, their land and people having been taken away."

Listening to him, I thought of Jesus' words in the Gospel of

Matthew. In the Garden of Gethsemane, during the hour when Jesus was betrayed and arrested, Peter struck off the ear of the servant of the high priest in order to protect his Lord. But Jesus tells him to stop. "Put your sword back in its place," Jesus said to him, "for all who draw the sword will die by the sword." Or as Martin Luther King Jr. once said, "Violence begets violence."

The next question on the conference call came from a woman in Colorado. She was baffled by all the paperwork and assignments we had to do just to start the day in the morning, many of which seemed repetitious. Lynn laughed and said, "Well, how can one teach an extraordinarily sacred, oftentimes abstract process in a pragmatic material world to someone who is not even there with you? How do you explain things that are part of the unknowable? You do that through the process of experience. The fact that you come against doing the work and that you don't like it is because it's changing you and it's important."

Lynn said that there is an aspect in each and every one of us that does not want to grow, that does not want to learn about the unknowable because we can't explain it in words and it's not part of the ordinary world. So we prefer not to do the personal work and instead to do Native ceremony, like dragging buffalo skulls around the flowering tree, the sun dance, which was done in a magnificent manner mostly by the Lakota and the Cheyenne.

"We're not doing that ceremony because we're battling ignorance," she said. "But to battle ignorance, you don't make yourself strong in the same way that a warrior would who's going to be carrying a spear or a bow and arrow into battle. You are making yourself strong for the supreme battle, the battle of wills, the battle of light and darkness, the battle of ignorance and complete universal awareness. You are becoming a healer. It's not A plus B equals C. It's very different.

"When you are creating something new, which is a new you, somebody who can go out into the world and choreograph the energies in the universe and step up to the plate and really mean something in the world, you have to be strong, not only physically, but spiritually. Does this make sense to you?"

"Yes, it does make sense that I need to do all this to learn the abstract thing," said the caller. "What I don't understand is that it seems to overlap, and I don't know the difference between doing a wheel and doing a *Face of the Altar.*"

"Oh my God, the difference is enormous. I tell you what, I understand it's a different way of teaching, honey, and I understand that it is a circular process, not an up-the-ladder process, and at some point you just have to trust me. You have to trust in the infinite extraordinary wisdom of your teacher and the Sisterhood of the Shields that we know what we're doing. This school is an unbelievable gift because it will take you to where you want to go. And each and every one of you is going to go to a different place, and you are going to arrive at a place of reckoning, a place where you become miraculous and outstanding and you live a magical life, more so than you ever have before."

The moderator asked if anyone else had questions. I had toiled with the idea of asking Lynn, "Can we quicken things up to speed the process of transformation?" But when I tried to raise this question, I was unable to speak. Lynn had provided us with such powerful information that everything seemed self-explanatory or on the verge of revealing itself.

Chapter 6
STOLEN INHERITANCE

After the library, I took my children to Burger King. They played in the play area as I sat at the booth and read school material. The phone rang. It was one of my sisters. She skipped the word hello and, with an urgent voice, said, "I just found out that Luke sold our grandfather's land!"

"How do you know?"

"He admitted it."

"How?"

"He always said there were two land properties that belong to us," she said. "But today we found out that's not true. Our two aunts said there are three properties of land. When my husband confronted him about this, Luke admitted he sold the third property."

I stared absentmindedly through the window. "All these years he has been telling us lies."

"I can't believe it. He acts like he's a saint, like he's too honest for his lips to utter a white lie. And yet he's not only a big liar, but also a thief!"

"I'm surprised he admitted to it."

"Well, he saw that we kept coming back to him about the land, asking him where the property deeds are. Then our aunts got involved."

"He felt cornered."

"You should see how he talked to me," she said, her voice now trembling. "He's acting as cool as a chicken's ass, like I'm making a big deal of everything and what he did is no real crime. He said he needed the money to come here."

"How much did he sell the land for?"

"He won't say."

We fell silent for a moment. Baffled, I watched my kids climb the play area's netted step entrance, crawl into the tunnels, and come down the slide that bends.

"What should we do now?" she asked.

"What's there to do? He stole the money and he'll never give it back. The only thing we can do is cut off contact with him."

"But I want my share!"

"How are you going to get it?"

"I don't know, but there must be a way."

We again fell into a moment of silence as we reviewed the situation.

"How can a person do such a thing when here I am, even when I do the right thing, I'll sometimes doubt myself?" she asked.

Her words saddened me. It did feel like sometimes being honest and good did not pay off.

"Let's think this over before we jump into any rash decisions," I said, and after we hung up, I called another sister who I often turned to for family advice.

"So what's going to be his punishment?" she asked after I updated her on what happened. "Do you guys want to cut off ties with the family?"

"It looks like that's all we can do."

I remained at Burger King, sat at the booth, and watched my children play. My coffee had turned as cold as a Coca-Cola, but I continued to drink it as I marveled at how someone like my cousin so easily took what was not his when I didn't even know how to take what was rightfully mine. For years I worked for free, doing a service to the community just like my father had done. By day, he was the head of the accounting department at the railway station, but in his free time, he offered several free services: he was a bonesetter, a translator, a money lender to people who often did not repay him, and in court he represented people who could not afford an attorney.

The concept of giving is good, but when it is done at the expense of your dreams or your family's wellbeing, or when it reaches a point where people are taking advantage of you, then it is a self-worth issue. Lessons of discernment and setting boundaries must be learned. Otherwise, the flaws of the stories we grow up with will continue to haunt us and repeat themselves, preventing us from growing in our relationships and careers.

I did not want the financial situation my father put us in to repeat itself with the next generation. So I spent the next couple of weeks tied up with the stolen land's affairs, calling the Iraqi Embassy in Washington and visiting the local Iraqi Consulate to understand our rights. Luke made the situation worse by claiming he had sold the land for only two hundred dollars because the mujahedeen had threatened to kill him and his sister because they worked for the US Army as translators.

His story made no sense. First, he had brothers in the United States who had been generous with him for decades. Whenever he needed money, they sent it to him, few questions asked. Had his life and his sister's life been on the line, his American brothers would have belched a couple of hundred dollars to rescue them. Second, land was cheap during the sanctions, not after the war. After the war, when he began working for the US

Army, prices skyrocketed. The only thing you could buy for two hundred dollars was a few bricks, maybe, or a palm tree.

He said he had proof of the sale, and after some time, sent us a copy of a paper stamped by the trade commission which stated that the land was sold in 2002, before the war, when life in Iraq was safe for Christians, for 300,000 dinars. First, the proper department to have stamped this sale would have been the agriculture commission, not the trade commission. Second, 300,000 in dollar terms equated to a lot less than two hundred dollars. Luke's brother, Saul, who was also deceived, took this paper and flaunted it to the community.

"Prosecute him! Put his ass in jail!" said Peter, excitedly jumping off the brown couch as his half-a-dozen caged birds chirped in the background and his parrot shouted, *Hello! Hello!*

Peter was a short, stout, and hefty man who rarely discussed a topic without putting his whole heart and body into it. His animated character caused everyone to sit and watch and to listen with complex auditory and visual processing. His wife Angel, who was Luke's sister, was the exact opposite. She was tall and slender and had a passive attitude toward almost all situations. If someone fell from the roof, for instance, Peter would bounce up and down at the occasion, yelling so loud the police would hear him miles away so he would not need to trouble himself to call them. Angel, on the other hand, would rush to the fallen person to see if they were dead or alive and treat their injuries.

After Peter suggested that his brother-in-law Luke be prosecuted and his ass put in jail, Angel bit into a pita sandwich and asked ever so gently, "No, why say that?"

"I don't care! I don't give a fuck! He deserves it! Lock him up in jail!"

Peter and Angel had invited some of the family, including me, my sister, and her husband, Saul, who was also Luke's brother, to their house to mediate the situation. We said we'd come on the condition that Luke was not present. No one could stand the sight of him, not only because he had deceived us, but because he showed no remorse. He behaved as if he'd done nothing but accidentally break a china cup. When one of my sisters suggested that, as retribution, he forego his rights over the remaining two lands, he replied, "What right do you have to tell me to forego my portion of my grandfather's land?"

"Wasn't it enough that you already took what wasn't rightfully yours?" she asked.

He was upset that she had an *attitude* with him and told her he could not communicate with someone giving him an *attitude* and raising their voice at him. It was not proper, after all, he said. So we decided we did not want to sit with someone who was so proper.

"I know he made a mistake," Angel said, cracking a popular Middle Eastern red dyed seed I knew not from which fruit it came. "But we can't focus on that and forget all the good things he has done."

"You keep calling what he did a mistake," I said, "but this was not a mistake. It was premeditated. He spent time creating fake papers, conspired with others to be witnesses in front of the city clerk. He continued with this lie for ten years until we caught him, and now he presents us with a fraudulent paper that says he sold the land for less than two hundred dollars."

"He even stooped as low as blaming his deceased brother for having sold the land," my sister said.

"You keep asking that we not forget the good things," I said.

"What are those good things?"

"I'm with you guys!" Peter jumped in once again. "He's an asshole! I agree! Prosecute him!"

"*Habbibi*, that's not the way to go about…."

"I don't give a fuck! He deserves it!"

"We don't want to hurt anyone," Saul said. "We just want the original deeds to the land."

"He said he would get them for you guys," she said.

"He's been saying that for years, but then nothing!"

"And after all he has done, he's going behind our backs talking shit about us to our other cousins, spreading rumors and lies," my sister said.

Angel remained quiet.

"Can I have more tea?" my sister asked.

"Oh, sure." Angel left the table.

"His ass deserves to be in jail, but at the same time, the guy should have the chance to defend himself," said Peter, who had somehow composed himself. "In court, that's what they do."

"Here's the problem with that," I said. "Your wife's family has the tendency of doing something wrong and thinking they can fix it with a smile and an explanation. They've done this for years, but now it's just on a much larger scale. Still, they want to use the same method of smiling and saying, 'Oh, I didn't know. I made a mistake. I meant no harm. We're God loving people.' Then they go on and surprise us with another so-called 'mistake,' and we're supposed take the same bullshit excuses for an excuse."

He shrugged, like, *yeah, that's true.*

"We don't hate him or wish him ill will or expect to never talk to him again," I said. "But he wants to erase his wrongdoing with fancy words and an angelic look, the very attributes which he used to fool us in the first place. He wants to force us into forgiving him the way he wants it done. So far, he has not even had the patience to let us get over the shock of how he has deceived us. He goes around and calls relatives, whom he never even met, who don't even live in this state, spreads rumors, and causes more problems."

"You're right, and I'm sick of this!" Peter bellowed, ripping off the composure and jumping to his feet again. "This is creating a wedge between the families, and I can't handle it anymore. I told my wife, we don't need this crap! Fucking prosecute him! And you know the other day some guy called and said to my wife, 'Get your sister out of Iraq. What is she doing in the village of Telkaif all alone without family? People are talking.'"

"Have you guys tried to get her out?" I asked, concerned.

"Yeah, but she won't listen," Angel said, returning with the tea kettle. "She's stupid. We tried everything, even pretended that our mother was dying and her last wish is to see her before she dies. She said, 'Oh, I'll talk to Mom on the phone and put her heart at ease.' We said she's in the hospital, she can't talk on the phone. She wants you to come see her. Nothing!"

"Who is this guy that called you?" I asked.

"I don't know," she said. "It was a number from back home that we don't recognize. He had called me a few times before saying similar things. I told him never to call me again."

I calmly drank my coffee and thought this matter over. "What if his intentions are to kidnap her and hold her for ransom? You know how these criminals do that with Christians who have families in America, figuring their families have money?"

Peter laughed sarcastically. "Huh! If any motherfucker calls me to give ransom money for her, I'd say, kill the fucking bitch!

It's her fault for not leaving Iraq!"

With that last statement, the meeting was adjourned.

Chapter 7
THE PATH TO ENLIGHTENMENT

Monday, May 13, marked twenty-seven years since my dad passed away. Lynn's phone conference was scheduled for 8 pm. As I prepared for the call, he came to mind along with my oldest sister, who passed away not long after he did. Lynn opened with a prayer, and then the moderator began to read the questions. I did not hear what the first question was, my thoughts still with my father, but I did hear Lynn's response. She said, "I don't think that any one path is the correct way to enlightenment. Shamanism is a great way to learn. It's one way of doing that, of reaching enlightenment, of feeling free and feeling utter joy."

Another person asked her what she meant by going into the dream.

"Part of it is understanding the mystery and knowing your life is a true miracle," she said. "You cannot really explain what power is. Power allows you to follow your dreams. But first you have to know what that dream is."

I was trying to catch up with writing the answer when someone else asked, "What is double dreaming?"

"Double dreaming is about holding and protecting your energy in daily life and not wasting your energy in things that don't concern you, like gossip and such," she said. "I do think that ninety percent of the people in the world have been abused

65

at a young age in one way or another, and so you end up hindering your own sacred dreams."

"The most difficult things for me is to be heard in the ordinary world," another caller said.

"The school helps you to be heard not just by others listening to you, but by you listening to yourself," said Lynn. "You have to do that in order to create a mirror for yourself, for your act of power. We're peeling away the clouds of ignorance that cloud your vision. Then you begin to see that you really do have something important and wonderful to say, and more and more you're appreciating yourself. Patience and diligence are important in this."

"The next question was sent by Weam from Michigan," said the moderator. "She writes, 'In one of Lynn's books, Agnes tells Lynn that there are people who are so enlightened, they can manifest their dreams within no time. They don't have the long gaps that ordinarily take place with others. My question is, can one speed up that relationship between a thought and its manifestation and if so, how?'"

I had not asked that question during the last conference call, but it had continued to stalk me, so I asked it during this conference call.

"The way you speed up the process to enlightenment is don't be impatient," Lynn said. "We all want things to happen instantly. We need to be patient. I mean that in a shamanic way. Shamanic rests with patience. It's about not doing and preserving your energy so it becomes like a battery." She said a few other things, and then forgot what the question was.

The moderator repeated it.

Lynn laughed. "Yeah, well, when you figure out how to reach enlightenment faster, can you tell me?"

I laughed.

"You can learn quicker with a teacher who has been there before you," Lynn said. "The faster you get rid of your mental conditions, the more you do the exercises, the more the negativities will be cleared away. So, aspects of yourself can more quickly turn into your dreams. Impatience is a block. It's like trying to move the current of a river a certain way and instead clogging it up. You can ruin the effect. You want to become like a piece of bamboo, where energy flows freely through you. Right now you are getting in the way of the Great Spirit. Get out of the way. Great Spirit knows what you want and what you need. Part of the block is being dissatisfied with the personal power that you already have."

The answer was incredibly satisfying. My impatience was slowing me down. That was all this was. I thanked Lynn for her answer and the moderator moved right along to an apprentice who was frustrated with the resistance she had toward the work.

"I'm not lazy, but I'm scared," she said.

"Attaining your power means going into unknown territory, so you need to be brave. You are like an iceberg, and as you near enlightenment you begin to melt and you're afraid of that."

The last question was from an apprentice who felt jealous of a more accomplished colleague at work. This feeling of jealousy bothered her.

"Jealousy is not about love," said Lynn. "It's about restrictions and lack of self-worth."

"Why do we have jealousy?" the caller asked.

"We want to bring people to our level because we haven't gotten to where they are. It's a mirror. See if you can find a way to honor that, then get rid of the jealousy and learn something from it. Bring jealousy to the heart because the heart doesn't know jealousy. Heart only knows love and when you bring it to the heart, jealousy transforms to love."

The questions were done. Lynn said the closing prayer and before she let us go, she said to be sure to utilize her. "Use me! Squeeze me like a sponge. I'm here for you."

I wished I could move in with her, the way she had been able to move in with her teachers. That idea was funny, however, since I could not get to the two four-day gatherings held each year, let alone go off and live with her. I could schedule a call, but what would I say during the call? There was nothing to say, except for thank you, and oh yes, this work is sometimes quite difficult. Looking into our shadow selves was frightening.

Carl Jung wrote in *On the Psychology of the Unconscious*:

> It is a frightening thought that man also has a shadow side to him, consisting not just of little weaknesses and foibles, but of a positively demonic dynamism. The individual seldom knows anything of this; to him, as an individual, it is incredible that he should ever in any circumstances go beyond himself. But let these harmless creatures form a mass, and there emerges a raging monster.

That monster emerged whenever my deceased sister came to mind to tell me that maybe, just maybe, what happened to her would end up happening to me.

* * *

When we lived in a small ranch home on Masch Street in the mid-1980s, most nights the seven of us, my siblings and I, gathered on one bed, where we told stories, joked, laughed, and, on a few occasions, watched two in the crowd get into a serious discussion then physically wrestle on the bed and fall over to the floor. One day in particular we went through a stack of old pictures. We roared with laughter at the men decked out in 1970s shaggy moptop hairstyles, dressed in bellbottoms and disco shirts. We admired the women in miniskirts, cropped pants, and fancy updos.

Iraqi women who grew up in the 1950s, 60s, and 70s had much more liberty than the women who grew up during the 80s and the 90s. They enjoyed higher education, independence, and positions in the public workforce. Many dressed in miniskirts and bikinis. In fact, in our neighborhood, almost every home had some sort of bathing attire because the families had a membership to Al Zawraa Swim Club. This made it useful when an out-of-towner who did not possess a bathing suit was invited for a swim, as so happened with my cousin Bushra.

My sisters told me the story.

One day Bushra spent the night over our house. The next day, my sisters offered to take her to the swimming pool. She explained that she did not have a bathing suit. They offered to lend her theirs. She said, "You are thin. I am fat. How will I fit into your bathing suits?"

My sisters went to the neighbor's house, where a bigger sized woman lived, to borrow a bathing suit. Three of my sisters then surrounded Bushra, trying to help squeeze the bathing suit up her body. They instructed her to lean to the left, lean to the right, press her palms against the walls, lift her leg this and that way, thread her arm through the strap, hold in her breath and tummy, etc. The women received a good workout before the bathing suit fully went up my cousin's curvy body. The same process had to be repeated at the pool's locker room. Then came the swimming part.

Al Zawraa had two pools outside, one for children and one for adults. Bushra did not know how to swim, so one of my sisters led her into the children's pool, told her to hold onto the edge, and taught her how to kick her legs and arms. After a while, my sister left her and joined the others in the adult pool. Bushra continued to kick and paddle like a penguin until she looked around and saw people laughing at her. She realized she was the only non-child in the pool. She got out, jumped into the adult pool, and hollered, "I'm drowning! I'm drowning!"

My sisters rushed to her rescue. One of them told her, "Bushra, why are you drowning? You can reach the floor."

"I know," she said, smiling as she landed on her feet. "I was playing you just like you played me by having me look like a fool in the children's pool."

When Khairallah Talfah, Saddam's paternal uncle and his father-in-law and the brother-in-law of then President Al-Bark, became the Mayor of Baghdad in the early 1970s, he ordered the security service and police force to spray-paint the legs of any woman wearing short skirts and to tear the bellbottom trousers worn by any male or female. These actions against any Westernized contemporary trends only lasted a few weeks and were terminated abruptly, when Vice President Saddam Hussein intervened. These trendy fashions subsequently spread all over the country and ironically had been worn even by Tulfa's own sons and daughters.

My siblings and I laughed so hard at Bushra's story, most of our bodies hung out of the bed like puppets. I then came across a picture of a woman sitting on a nice large bed, wearing a white gown. She was peculiar looking, as skinny as a string bean and with very dark skin. She could have passed for an African woman, but her hair did not have the Afro-texture. She resembled those malnutritioned women they showed on television commercials that try to raise money for Africa.

"Who is this?" I asked my sister Nidhal, wondering why she would preserve a picture of a complete stranger.

Nidhal quietly looked at me then looked at the others sitting on and around the bed. Something was wrong. This was not an African woman, I realized, and soon we all knew who this was. This was Basima, the sister who was diagnosed with muscular dystrophy ten years ago. Because she lived in Iraq, we had no idea how badly it had sucked her blood, turned her from a beautiful woman to a corpse.

My oldest sister Basima was so full of grace and beauty that when she walked the streets of Baghdad, people mistook her for the famous Egyptian actress Soad Hosny, known as the "Cinderella of Egyptian cinema." She got married when she was eighteen years old. Her husband did not have much at first, but as time went on, and after the birth of a daughter and son, he became a wealthy man. One day, he took his family to London, where his daughter had to have heart surgery. While there, my sister went to see the doctor for pain she had in her hands. They did some tests, and she was diagnosed with muscular dystrophy.

Her husband wanted to bring her to the United States for treatment and so that she could be with her family. He made an official request from Saddam and was told that unfortunately, as this disease had no cure, there was no sense in going anywhere for treatment. However, if he could get a letter from a doctor stating they had a cure for it, Saddam would permit her to go. No doctor we went to was willing to say that because it would be a lie. There was no cure.

My family was devastated, and yet all they could do was get excited when volunteers for the Muscular Dystrophy Association appeared at our door to collect money, or when we gathered around the television for the Jerry Lewis Labor Day Telethon. We would watch as millions upon millions of dollars were raised and thought, this should do it! This should help find a cure for our sister. She will be well again and will be able to raise her children.

Year after year, millions were raised, and my sister got worse and worse. She was confined to a wheel chair, then a bed.

"I never told you what happened when I arrived to Baghdad," Nidhal said.

After relatives picked Nidhal up from Baghdad airport, they drove her to Basima's house, where she'd be staying. Nidhal entered the house and was shocked by what she saw. The Basima who people mistook for the most beautiful actress in Egypt was now all bones. Nidhal yelled and cursed everyone for not having informed her of my sister's condition. She ran into one of the nearby rooms, shut the door, and wept for hours.

"I brought this picture to prepare anyone who might end up going to Iraq," she said. "I didn't want you guys to experience the same shock that I did."

Grief suddenly absorbed the air in the room and, as if we were at a funeral, we mourned over the deterioration of a loved one. We realized that the friendly volunteers who came knocking on our door and Jerry's umpteen telethons could do us no good. Our sister was nearly gone, and if God had any mercy on her, he would take her away altogether. Soon after, He did just that.

After my sister was diagnosed with muscular dystrophy,

during the ten years she suffered the disease and after she died, I would hear stories about how evil eyes, otherwise known as jealous people, followed her like a radar. She was married to a handsome and now rich husband, had two beautiful children, and carried an extraordinary feminine aspect that made others feel like her life had accelerated at an amazing pace.

A few incidents, people say, forewarned of her tragedy. Once, as she took a shower, the water heater in the bathroom blew up, nearly ending her life. In the second incident, during the Iraq-Iran war, a missile hit right beside her home. In the Eastern world, the count of three leads to a disaster. In the Western world, three is a charm.

The last phone conversation I had with Basima, she made one request. She said in a quavering voice, "Don't get married until my daughter comes to America."

"Don't worry, I'll wait," I said, not having plans, at sixteen years old, to marry anytime soon.

I did not understand why she had made that request until I was a lot older and realized she wanted me to help her daughter excel and worried that marriage would disable me from doing just that. Her wish never came true. Her daughter ended up getting married before me and eventually moved to Australia.

When my first-year mentor Leslie said she felt that I had a fear of success, her words did not ring true. But during my second year, while working on one of the school assignments, the story of my deceased sister resurfaced and I saw that subconsciously I feared that success came at a big price. If I make it, does it mean something bad might happen to me or a family member? If I remain where I am, at least I can secure the health and love which were most dear to me. There was a seed buried within me that believed one could not complement the other.

That, coupled with the fear I had of failure, of following in my father's footsteps and losing the house because I did not have enough resources to do the last touches, were the perfect mixture for sabotaging my career.

Chapter 8

A Secret Story

"Fiona, there's something I need to tell you before you go," I said reluctantly and with a strange fear creeping inside of me.

"Tell me the mystery," she said.

"I hadn't planned to say anything, but I can't help it. This is tormenting me, and since I can't share it with anyone else, so not to worry them, I don't know what to do."

I began my story, which went back to how my husband and I met.

My husband and I met in Iraq, during my trip in 2000. The aunt whom I stayed with, Aunt Katrina – everyone called her Katina, without the r – had done an excellent job keeping suitors at bay. Although I'd heard rumors about which men were interested in me, no one dared approach me directly about this matter. They went through the elders, like my aunts, and so I myself was never bothered. What bothered me were the dinner invitations that would not stop. In Michigan, I was accustomed to having coffee for breakfast, coffee for lunch, and a home-cooked meal when I got home around 5 pm. In Baghdad, people were serious about having three meals a day and a brunch somewhere in between. If you skipped a meal, they took offense. I skipped meals anyway, or ate lightly, which was also offensive.

Their hospitality was, at times, overwhelming because in the Arab world when a person, especially a traveler, is invited to a meal, the table is stacked with enough food to feed a village, even if the hostess barely has enough to feed her family. The warmth and kindness they exuberate makes it difficult to say, "No, thank you," when, for instance, a tray of baklava is pressed toward your chest, followed by a box of chocolates. After two and a half weeks of such fussing, I finally told my aunt, "No more dinner invitations!"

"But your cousins Reja and Salman want to have you over for dinner," she said.

"No! I will not go!"

"Just this one last time," she said. "For my sake."

I tried to wiggle myself out of this, but I could not disappoint my aunt. She'd reminded me so much of my mother that on a few occasions, I'd even accidentally called her "Mom." I liked Reja and her husband Salman, both cousins of mine and cousins to each other, which made the relationship even closer, and I realized a felony would occur if I declined their invitation. I went and, as expected, the table was set with elaborate Iraqi appetizers, salads, and half a dozen main meal dishes.

Shortly after I arrived, two men showed up. They were Reja's nephews, which made them my half-second cousins. They were brothers and not much younger than Reja. Tall and on the thin side, but not skinny, they had a dark complexion, a moustache, and a dimple in their chins. They were more manly than handsome, and their manliness was elegant. At first I thought they were twins, but later I learned that one was a little older and married. The brothers sat with us for an hour or so and then excused themselves. I never saw them again.

The day of my departure from Iraq, as people came in and

out to bid me farewell, before my travel chaperone came to pick me up, my aunt pulled me aside. "Your cousins want to have a word in private with you," she said.

I went into the dining room, where eight to ten people were gathered around the table. I recognized all of them, but I didn't remember the names of at least half of them. They had me sit at the head of the table. A blonde haired, green eyed woman around my age sat closest to me.

"We are here to inform you that Sudaid is interested in you," she said.

"Who's Sudaid?" I asked.

"Reja's nephew. He was at her house the other day, when you were there."

"There were two men."

"The one that's not married."

"I couldn't tell them apart," I said.

Everyone was confused, evidently so accustomed to the two brothers that they could easily tell them apart. But they had no way of describing the difference in their features.

"Sudaid comes from a very good family, you can ask any-one," she said. She was married to the look-alike brother. "He has a bachelor's degree from Baghdad University, and his family is quite well off. He asked us to tell you he's interested in talking with you."

Everything started to make sense. It was a bit odd that my relatives were successful at preventing all suitors from knocking on my door. True, my mother had explicitly told my aunt before I came to Iraq that I had no intentions of getting married and not to try to convince me otherwise. Still, I was surprised they didn't take the liberty, as often happens with a tribal family, to ignore her. I was not aware that all this time there was talks of marriage, planning, and plotting. My relatives had come to an agreement and reserved their matchmaking energy and conspiracies for one particular family with two age-appropriate unwed sons whom they felt were worthy of me. Of the two, Sudaid took interest.

What didn't make sense was how I didn't detect that the men had come over that night with the intent to check me out. Because it was a family set-up, the degree of respect was at its highest, so I had no warning signs – aside from my cousin seeing a tall and handsome suitor in my Turkish coffee cup grains.

"I'm not interested in getting married," I said.

"He just wants to talk," said the blonde haired woman.

"How? I'm leaving today for America."

"You two can talk on the phone."

A simple solution, I thought. During the Baath regime, the telephones were monitored 24/7 by the government and the duration of the phone calls was limited, anywhere from five to twenty minutes. When we called relatives in Iraq, we avoided the subject of the United States altogether so as not to raise suspicion that that relative had any intention of fleeing the country. We spoke Aramaic so an Arabic person wouldn't understand what was being said or we used words that meant something else, like, "We're sending you pistachios and almonds with this one guy that's coming to visit us in April," meaning we're attempting to flee in April.

Often those monitoring the phone lines simply got bored and popped into the conversation like a jack-in-the-box. One day I was telling my niece, who is six months older than me, how beautiful she is, and she said, "No, you're more beautiful." We went back and forth like that, emphasizing each other's qualities, when suddenly a man interrupted us. "No need to argue, ladies," he said in a sexy voice. "I'm sure you're both equally beautiful."

She and I laughed and I turned red with embarrassment.

"I can't agree to anything, especially since I am here alone without my family," I said to the woman making the marriage proposition. "I must return home the same way I came."

She paused. "That's appropriate, but can you think it over once you're home?"

"Yes, I will," I lied, simply wanting this meeting to end.

After I returned to Michigan, my cousins called me several times. I never answered when I saw an "unknown number" on the caller ID. My mother answered, and I could hear her from the kitchen on the first floor explaining how I had come as a young girl to America and was too Americanized to marry without getting to know the guy through courting. I laid on my bed and thought about the exhausting trip to Iraq.

My cousins in Iraq finally gave up trying to convince me to talk to Sudaid. Four years went by, during which time Sudaid migrated to the United States on his own. He later told me that one day he was driving down my street when his aunt in the passenger seat pointed toward my house and said, "That's Weam's home."

"Did she get married?" he asked, recalling the day we'd met.

"No."

"Can you call to see if she'll speak to me now?"

"She's two years older than you!"

"I don't care if she was ten years older," he said.

We ended up getting married, and I filed an I-130 petition for him. Then on January 30, 2006, we had an interview appointment with a Mrs. Jones at the Immigration and Naturalization Service (INS) building in Detroit. The INS building was the same as when I first came to it in 1989, at age eighteen, to take my naturalization exam. People of all national backgrounds – Pakistani, Arab, French, Mexican – filled the rows of seats. The place had the smell of other countries' spices. Dozens of different languages bounced into the air and tickled our ears. I liked listening to foreigners speak their native tongue, because then it became a melody which only the listener could define.

I was not the same woman I was when I was given ten questions about the United States and asked to write a sentence or two in English before I was handed a paper showing I passed the test. Back then I had on a shirt that accentuated my tiny waist. Today I was wearing maternity clothes and I had on the diamond cross my husband presented me with on the day of our *kilma*, which translates to "word" but really means "a promise." It's a ceremony prior to the engagement where, in front of close family, the man presents his future fiancée with a piece of jewelry to show they are spoken for each other. Sudaid had on his navy suit, reminding me of my father who used to love dressing in suits when going out. He also had on the gold cross his parents gave him.

Our appointment was at nine o'clock. As we waited our turn, we watched one foreigner after another get called to go behind a portable wall and later come out with a big smile and a certificate in hand. We watched a little Arabic girl play. We chit chatted with her parents. The clock read one, and we began to get impatient. Sudaid had to be at work at three o'clock and I at four. We made small talk to pass the time but soon a discomforting feeling took over. We decided to call into work, but since phones were not allowed to enter the building, we went outside to our car to use our cell phones.

At five o'clock, the waiting area was empty. We were the only ones left. Mrs. Jones, a large black woman, appeared and called my name. Sudaid and I were so relieved, we forgot all the hours of waiting. She led us to a small cubicle which, with the size of my belly, I had difficulty fitting into. Before we sat down, Mrs. Jones asked Sudaid in a dry tone, "Did you know that you're out of status in this country?"

"We received notice from his attorney only yesterday that he lost the political asylum case," I said, searching for the letter in my purse. "The letter said we had ten days to appeal."

"Don't matter. He's still out of status for now. Plus, I asked him, not you."

Her tone and her eyes were sharp, demeaning, and intimidating. I was stunned and did not know how to respond. Under any other circumstance, like if I was at Macy's or Kroger, McDonald's or Starbucks, and the cashier or salesperson spoke to me in that manner, I would have asked for the manager. The manager would patiently hear my complaint, apologize about me having a bad experience, and settle the matter in a civilized manner to ensure I would remain a returning customer, maybe offer a free ice cream or a 25 percent discount on clothing apparel. To a corporation, I was somebody. The confidence in Mrs. Jones' voice assured me I ought to remain quiet. Any peep and my life could turn upside down.

"Did you bring the necessary documents?" she asked without looking at us.

I handed her a large envelope which included, among other things, my husband's new employment authorization card. She took the employment card and sliced it in half with a scissor.

"He won't need that since he's out of status," she said.

I did not know what that meant. My husband and ten others were paroled into the United States by the Secretary of Homeland Security. The Chaldean Church was involved in the process. Once he was in the US, he applied for political asylum. We got married a year and a half after he was here, while his asylum case was still under review. Only the day prior did we learn he was denied political asylum. But our appointment had nothing to do with the political asylum case. We were supposed to be interviewed about our marriage.

"Our marriage is in good faith," I said, maintaining my composure, although I was afraid. "I brought our engagement and wedding videos…"

"I don't need to see those," she interrupted. "How would I view them? I don't have a video player."

I began praying, even while I explained to Mrs. Jones how my husband and I had a lavish engagement party at a banquet hall with 150 guests, and a priest doing the ceremony, as is customary in our culture. Later we had a lavish wedding of 300 guests. I had the receipt of the reception to prove it.

She glanced over the receipts and shuffled through the papers like a bored child would with a deck of cards. "I'll need an affidavit from you."

"When I called the 800 number, they said I didn't need to…"

"You can't count on those 800 numbers for accurate information," she said. "I also need more proof that you two are married. Don't you have bills that are in both your names?"

I wanted to point out my pregnant belly, but I pointed to the mortgage papers. "We bought our house together."

She was uninterested and continued avoiding our eyes. "You need further proof."

Two white men, one tall and another one short, appeared outside the cubicle.

"These men are with Homeland Security," said Mrs. Jones. "As of now, your husband is considered out of status and his case is with them."

We were escorted to another part of the building.

"Ma'am, you can sit in the waiting area," one of the men said. He then turned to my husband. "We just have a few questions for you."

"Don't be scared, this is normal procedure," Sudaid said to me before he was taken behind two large doors.

His words did not fool or soothe me. Many Iraqis I knew married men and women from Iraq and, when it was time for the I-130 interview, the process went as smooth as butter. Of course, that was mostly before 9/11.

I sat, and waited, and watched an attorney with a large suitcase busily exchange words with a woman with three small children, Romanian I presumed. He told her that authorities had taken her husband to the airport to be deported. I recalled Monica, the Romanian cleaning lady that twice a week came into the real estate office where I once worked. One day Monica came in crying. Her fiancé was caught drinking and driving and detained in an immigration prison. Two weeks later he called her from the airport to inform her he was being deported.

The short officer came out. "I just want to let you know this will take half an hour or so."

I thanked him and three hours later, I still sat there. I'd forgotten that I was seven months pregnant and had had nothing to eat since I woke up this morning. My husband and I planned to have breakfast after the interview was over. The officer returned and apologized for the delay.

"We just have to get a clearance on him and that has to go through Washington," he said. "We've already sent his name out and are waiting for a response. Don't worry. Although we have the right to send him back, that probably won't happen."

He must have seen the terror in my face.

"You haven't heard of anyone being sent back to Iraq, have you?" he asked.

He then disappeared through the doors and left me waiting for more hours. A dozen things went through my mind until darkness approached. I did not know what to do. I was afraid to leave the area, of not being there when someone came out to give me an update. Finally, I decided I would go look for Mrs. Jones. The cubicles were all empty. The only person around was the security guard, a black woman, at the building's entrance.

"Can you please contact someone from inside that room to let me go in and sit with my husband?" I asked.

"That's not possible," the guard said. "You'll have to wait until they come out."

"The lights are turned off! The place is closed!"

"You can wait in your car."

"It's the middle of winter. It's freezing outside."

"You can turn your car on."

"For how long? One, two, three hours?"

I walked away, feeling as if I was in a third-world country, where there were no laws against government officials mistreating citizens they disliked. When I was in Iraq, I accompanied my cousin to some office where the man sitting behind the desk, someone clearly of power, was insolent toward my cousin. My cousin just took it. I sensed my cousin's fear and felt sorry for him, thinking, if this happened in America, people wouldn't stand for it.

I returned to the empty waiting area and prayed that this night would end okay. The door later opened, and the short officer told me I could come inside. Inside looked like the cops quarters in movies. Sudaid sat behind one of the desks, which had piles of messy papers and a carryout of Chinese food. I sat on the chair facing him and we immediately held hands.

"Did they tell you what they want?" I asked.

"They've said nothing. This whole time I've just sat here, waiting."

"Have you eaten?"

He laughed. "I'm fine. What about *you*?"

"I'm not hungry. I won't have an appetite until you're out of here."

"Pretty soon, *habbibti*. Pretty soon. Just say, '*Ya Allah*.'"

I held back my tears. "I've been saying that."

He tried to make me smile, and soon the short officer returned. "We've been unsuccessful in getting a response from Washington. I'm afraid Sudaid will have to stay the night."

"But he didn't do anything wrong!" I jumped.

"I'm sorry, but that's the protocol. The background check must first go through the Washington office. Without their permission, we cannot let him go."

I looked at Sudaid pleadingly.

"It's okay, don't be scared!" he said, but his eyes were red.

"Please, isn't there anything we can do?" I asked the officer.

"I'm afraid not."

"Can I stay with him?"

"Don't worry. He'll be out tomorrow."

I was not convinced. This man had repeatedly made false promises. How did I know that these people, who were treating us like criminals, who thought us unworthy of being offered a glass of water, were not tricking me, that they would not deport my husband while I was all cozy in bed? Sudaid had already been in the United States three years, and he had dealt with the immigration court and INS repeatedly. Now, three years later, on the day of our interview, they decide to check his name and create drama?

We stood up and followed the officer into a hallway.

"I will call you early tomorrow morning," said the officer, handing me his business card. "You may exchange a quick goodbye with your husband."

He and the other officer stepped to the side. I stood in front of my husband. We didn't know when the next time we would see each other was. We said our "I love you's," and again my husband emphasized, "Don't be scared." He knew exactly what I was feeling because that was what he felt too. I turned to walk away. I didn't understand how my body was moving when all I wanted to do was remain and fight for his release.

I wept as I drove, to the point where my eyes got so blurry I feared causing an accident. At home, I got a quick bite to eat and ransacked the file cabinet to find bills with both our names on them, per Officer Jones' request. I clipped the Consumers Energy and the DTE Energy bills together and put them in an envelope. Then I took out my laptop, sat on the bed, and began to type the affidavit she requested. The baby kicked harder than usual. I took deep breaths I had learned in yoga practice and patted my stomach to help calm myself and the baby. It didn't work. The baby's kicks intensified and were painful.

It was five o'clock in the morning when I finished typing. My baby was still kicking. My stomach bulged up and down, left and right, sometimes so severely, I imagined the baby's hand or foot would tear the flesh and pop out. I set the laptop on the floor and fell asleep in the same clothes I'd worn to INS. In the morning, I called the number on the business card. No one answered. For the next couple of hours, I left dozens of messages, drank one coffee cup after another, forgot to eat, and received no responses. The phone rang, and I snatched it.

"How is Sudaid?" It was my husband's cousin.

"I don't know. I'm still waiting to see what happens."

"If you need anything, please let me know. And don't be afraid. Speak up for your rights. Remember, you're a US citizen."

Those words were strange to hear. The fact that he said them meant he knew about profiling and discrimination more than I did. I had been in America for over twenty-four years, spoke perfect English (well, most of the time), had American friends, teachers, and co-workers. I had always felt safe in this country up until the day prior, when the big bad wolf came out and lured me and my husband to a cubicle which we'd thought was the beginning of our freedom. In reality, it was a cage that went by the name of Homeland Security – although one would never guess that by looking at the website of friendly, smiley people. Overnight I no longer felt like an American citizen.

My sister called and suggested we go together to the immigration building. I drove. On the way there, she offered me *kleicha*, the national cookies of Iraq, which were plain, sprinkled with sugar, or filled with dates, walnuts, or coconut.

"I don't want to eat," I said, my eyes on the road.

"Take one," she insisted.

I glanced at the bag. "None have coconut, do they?"

"No."

I picked a plain one. Only when I bit into the *kleicha* did I realize how hungry I was. I ate four of them. My sister talked to me, mostly gossip, to keep me busy. It worked until we arrived at the building. I went to one of the cubicles and asked one of the employees if I could hand her an envelope which had my affidavit in it.

"You have to mail that," she said. "We can't take it here."

The instructions did say to mail the documents. It also advised that we not send them certified, as it might delay the immigration process. I didn't know which way to go. Send the package certified and risk the delay or send it uncertified and risk that it be lost.

"Don't worry about that for now," said my sister.

We went to the waiting area, where I'd sat alone the day before. I stopped a woman on her way toward the big doors. "Excuse me, ma'am, can you look up the status of my husband?"

She took his name and said she would be right back. A minute later the doors opened and my husband walked out with a huge smile on his face. He looked like an eagle ready to soar. I was incredibly happy and relieved, but also so tired and overwhelmed I thought I would pass out.

"Where did they take you?" I asked him in the car.

"To jail," he said, laughing. He put in an Arabic CD, turned the volume high, and drummed the palm of his hands against the steering wheel.

I lowered the volume. "Seriously?"

"Where did you think they were going to take me, a hotel?"

My sister and I looked at each other.

"What is that?" I asked, pointing to the band around his wrist.

"You don't believe me? I was arrested, baby!" And to the beat of the music, he did an Arabic clap – with fingers wide open, causing the palms to aggressively hit each other. "Got my picture taken, got fingerprinted, handcuffed, the whole shot!"

"Handcuffed?"

"What do you think? When you walked away last night, the short officer put handcuffs on me. I thanked him for waiting until you were gone. He's such a nice guy, he even apologized, said, 'Sorry man that I have to do this.'"

"Yes, he was nice," I said, though disturbed by all the details. "Then what?"

"They put me in a car with a bunch of other guys and took us to the county jail."

"Did you eat?"

"I couldn't. The floors were disgusting and so was the look of the food. I gave my tray to someone else there."

He took in a deep breath and said what he liked to say morning, day, and night, and several other times in between. "Thank God a thousand times!" He stopped at a red light. My sister offered him *kleicha*. He took the one filled with palm dates. "You know why all this happened? Because my name resembles the name of some other guy, a Saudi."

"Oh my God! Did they clear it up?"

"They said they did." He handed me papers entitled *Order of Deportation*. "I have to report to the Department of Homeland Security every month."

A discomforting feel crawled inside of me again.

At home, I cut the band around my husband's wrist and as he washed up, I closely observed the mug shot imprinted on it. His eyes in the picture were as red as a pomegranate. I placed the wrist band in a drawer next to my bed so I would never forget this incident. That night, my husband confided that he too had been scared, scared that he would not see me or our baby for a very long time.

Months passed by without hearing anything from Mrs. Jones. When my daughter was born in April, my husband and I both forgot about that frightening day in January at INS. We were happy and excited about the baby. "It's a Girl" balloons floated in our living room, and bouquets of flowers sat on our fireplace's sitting bench. A few days after I'd come home from the hospital my sister-in-law dropped my mom over so she could see the baby and be around in case I needed anything.

I was getting the mail when I saw a car pull into my driveway. Two men in suits, one young and tall, the other short and much older, approached me, identified themselves as the FBI, and asked for my husband.

"He's not home. He's at work." I paused. "Would you like to come in?"

"Yes, if that's okay."

They came in, and I sensed them observing the house – the wedding photo hanging on the wall, the baby picture, the basinet and balloons, the grandmother. They sat at the kitchen table. "We've come to see if Sudaid could help us track down terrorists," the younger one said.

"I doubt he knows anything, but you can ask him yourself tomorrow. He'll be here in the morning."

They didn't say much else and excused themselves. Only the younger man returned the next day. He sat with my husband around the kitchen table. I went into the living room and nursed my daughter.

"We heard about your situation with immigration," the FBI agent said. "We wanted to come and inform you that if you could provide us with any information on terrorists, we can help you out."

"I don't know any terrorists," Sudaid said.

The man tapped his hands lightly on the table. He looked at me and back at Sudaid. "Even if you know someone who knows someone or if you or they heard something, that information would really help us…and you."

"Honest, I know no one. Have you ever heard of Christian Iraqi terrorists?"

The agent was quiet.

Post 9/11 many people relied on the "I'm Christian" identity to lessen the tensions between them and the US government. Yet regardless of religion, terrorism in Iraq did not exist until 2003, when the borders were left unprotected by the US military, allowing major terrorist groups from all around the world to come and set camp in Iraq, then to recruit through force and with bribes. During the start of the war, Arabic news channels who reported incidences of terrorism in Iraq identified the terrorists as Moroccan, Yemeni, Egyptian, etc. Terrorism was bred in Iraq after 2003, which explains why none of the 9/11 hijackers were of Iraqi origin, nor had there been any major terrorists in history who carried the Iraqi nationality, except for the Dawa Party, which Saddam tried to annihilate in the 1980s and which the United States in 2003 welcomed into power with open arms. Saddam was then hung for his attempts to defeat this terrorist group that was run by Iranian extremists and that had tried to assassinate him as the president.

The agent again tapped his fingers on the table. "Well, if you do hear of anything, it could really help you out."

"Why would I need help? I came here legally, through parole. I applied for political asylum, then got married and started a family. I'm waiting a response on my I-130 petition."

The FBI agent saw there was no persuading my husband. He stayed just a little longer and then left. As soon as he was gone, I lit a candle beside the Virgin Mary statue.

Chapter 9
THE STORY CONTINUES

A woman from the Center for Human Rights and Global Justice of New York University School of Law wrote me an email not long after our encounter with the immigration officials. They were producing a documentary entitled *Americans on Hold,* which aimed to humanize the issue of delays in the naturalization process. Beyond providing an avenue for individuals to share their stories, they hoped that the film would increase social awareness of the issue and motivate a demand for accountability for the implementation and enforcement of these harmful policies.

"We were told about your experience and found your story very troubling," she wrote. "We believe that it gets directly to the heart of what our film is trying to show. As such, we would very much like to discuss with you the possibility of your participation in the film."

I stared at the email so intently it was as if I wanted to enter the screen and sit with the people in the Global Justice building, where it was safe to pour my heart out. Nearly two years had passed, and Officer Jones from immigration had not contacted us. Should I have not sent the affidavit certified? Was I allowed to call her and look into the delay, or would that only annoy her and cause her to further delay the process?

I'd attended several speeches and conferences earlier in the year, one where Senator Carl Levin talked about his attempt to provide visas for two groups of Iraqi refugees who, in Iraq, were singled out by extremists for helping Americans and religious minorities who have family connections in America.

"Senator Carl Levin was in Iraq a week ago," said Ramzi Dalloo at a meeting. "He met with the Chaldeans and Assyrians in Iraq – the refugees – and he wants a way to allow Iraqi refugees to come here to the United States. What's happening in Iraq is an ethnic cleansing. We have a major responsibility to these people since we were the ones who unleashed these circumstances in Iraq."

One of the things on their agenda was to speed up the FBI review of each application, which they said "takes forever." He and another speaker explained that since 2001, immigration law has increasingly been used to target individuals perceived to be Muslim, Arab, Middle Eastern, or South Asian as potential threats to national security. In 2003, the US Immigration and Naturalization Service (INS) ceased to exist, and its service and benefit functions were transferred to the newly created US Citizenship and Immigration Services (USCIS) within the Department of Homeland Security (DHS).

The sound of my daughter and husband waking up pulled me away from the email that looked like a rescue ship. I went into the kitchen, poured myself a fresh cup of coffee, and started to boil water for the tea. I grabbed cardamom seeds and chipped the shell of each one with my teeth before throwing them into the kettle. It was a cold, winter morning, but the sun was out. I returned to the bedroom, where my daughter was curled up beside her father. At nineteen months old, she still slept in our bed despite all the advice of my doctor and the books that gave instructions on how to break this pattern. The bed was as warm as a furnace, and I slipped in and hugged my little girl whose wild curls fell over her face.

I told my husband about the documentary. He said nothing. When I pressed, he said he would have to eat breakfast before discussing such matters, because he was too hungry to think right now. He told me to make eggs and *dibis* while he went to buy *samoon*, fresh diamond-shaped pocket bread we buy from the Iraqi bakery down the street. *Dibis* is date syrup. Date syrup cooked right on top of fried eggs is a famous traditional Iraqi breakfast. In Iraq breakfast is very important, but it had its downs during the wars and sanctions. Date syrup, a common ingredient, was not so common after Saddam ordered the clearing of millions of date palms in an effort to root out snipers during the Iran-Iraq War. It was even less common during the sanctions.

"What do you want to do?" he asked me after he'd returned from the bakery and we sat at the breakfast table. He dipped the hot bread in the date syrup and fed my daughter. "Do you think this would actually help us?"

I grabbed the TV control and lowered the volume of the Arabic news channel. "I can't hear you, the TV is so loud!"

"Babba! Babba!" My daughter pointed at the *geimar*, clotted cream, he'd also bought fresh from the Iraqi market. He made a clotted cream sandwich with a spread of apricot marmalade and helped her eat it.

"I don't know if it will help or *hurt* us," I said, and I left the table.

I could not bear this issue, yet I badly wanted to speak out, to use my American rights, the ones that were my strength before the incident at immigration took place. After that day, my husband had to report to the USICS building every month. The mornings he did were dreadful for the both of us. We worried we'd never see each other again. He always made sure to call me as soon as he left the immigration building to assure me everything was okay.

One day when I was pregnant with my second child, I noticed it was noon and I had not heard from him. I called his phone and it went straight to voicemail. I began to panic. I called dozens of numbers, was switched from one person to the next, and in the end broke down crying and hung up. I sat in the corner of my kitchen floor and wept. My daughter came and cuddled beside me, and I sunk my wet face in her long curls. The phone rang. I saw it was my husband's number. I nervously answered.

"Weam, what's wrong *habbibi*?"

I broke down again. "I thought something happened to you."

My husband and I did not discuss the immigration issue much, but it was a constant cloud over our heads. When the idea of the documentary *Americans on Hold* came about, we went over it a few more times, analyzing the pros and cons and the risks involved. In the end, we decided to seek a different route for help. I contacted Senator Carl Levin's office. A woman from his office responded promptly, and she immediately began looking into our case. After many attempts to contact Officer Jones, she was told that the file might be lost.

"Lost! How can a file get lost?"

"I'm still going over the matter with Officer Jones," the woman said. "Please bear with me."

Well, I bore it and bore it and one day I received a phone

call from the producer of *Americans on Hold*. I explained that if I didn't receive a positive response from the senator's office, I would then go through with the documentary if the producers had not by then gathered all the interviewees they needed. When I hung up the phone, I was unhappy that I'd passed up this opportunity. I wanted to go through with it, I really did, but I was afraid that such an action would cost my husband his stay in the US. I was behaving very un-American, but I had learned from Iraq, if you did not want to get into trouble with the government, you kept your mouth shut.

There were frequent phone calls and correspondence between us and the senator's office, but to no avail. Finally, we received a letter from Homeland Security explaining that a background check was a drawn-out and long process. By then, the total number of years that had passed since our visit with Officer Jones was four years, during which time I got pregnant and had a miscarriage and later got pregnant again and had a son.

"I don't understand it," I said, holding my six-month-old son in one arm. I showed my husband the letter. He sat on the couch, eating his late night chicken and potatoes dinner, my daughter right beside him and the sound of Al Jazeera News vibrating the house. "You have been in the United States for almost seven years. They've had your case for four years. But they're doing a background check?"

He did not look at the letter, but looked up at me. "Let's hire an attorney."

"An attorney! Why? People who have fake marriages got through this process barely knowing how to speak English."

"Well, with us, that's not how it is." He tried to feed my daughter a spoon of cucumber salad and got all upset. "How many times have I told you to put her hair back so she can see and eat?"

I went to look for an elastic hair band. When I returned, I put her hair in a ponytail and then sat on the floor, placing my son on my lap. "This isn't even legal under international law, you know. Why else would the Center for Human Rights do a report and documentary about it?"

"Look, I have nothing to hide. They want to check on me, let them. What I don't get is they already know everything about me, so…"

"They are wasting time on the wrong people!" I interrupted. "The Human Rights report says that undue delays in background checks are inefficient, ineffective, and counterproductive, that profiling can't be considered a reliable substitute for real intelligence work. It does not make us safer. It just produces fear, discrimination, and prejudice."

He stared at me for a moment. "We are getting an attorney."

"We can't afford an attorney!" I said, thinking of our mound of bills. Plus, we were in the middle of a great recession.

"We'll have to manage."

He and my daughter discussed what she wanted to eat next: the chicken, the potatoes, or the salad. She took pleasure in pointing at the food and watching him make it into small bites for her.

"Tens of thousands of Christian-Iraqi refugees are brought here in a short amount of time because of our involvement in the war," I said, almost as if talking to myself. "I understand that the refugees are displaced and need help, but where are my rights and those of my daughter and son as US citizens? How is it that Homeland Security spends less than a year doing background checks on people outside the country and with you, it is taking God knows how long?"

"We just have to accept the situation as it is."

"I can't!" I said. "I was not raised that way."

"So what's your answer?"

We looked at each other, him waiting, me not having an answer.

Despite my attempts to fight for our rights and our financial troubles, we ended up hiring an attorney. We just wanted some peace and closure on this matter. The attorney advised us to withdraw the old I-130 and open a new case. We received an interview date shortly after filing the new form. This time, the fact that the attorney was going to accompany us to the interview made us feel much safer.

We were very excited. My daughter's birthday was just a few days from the date of the interview, so we decided to plan a huge party. We invited both my family and my husband's family, anxious to break the good news to them at the birthday that our immigration problems were finally over. Two weeks before the interview, I received a message on my phone. It was Officer Jones, who had happily sliced my husband's employment card. It turned out she was not supposed to do that. She was calling, four years and two months later, to inform me of the following. "We've received some type of release on the I-130 petition and now need updated information for you and your husband – from 2006 on. You can either mail the information or drop it off at the Jefferson building."

She brought back the bitter memories, along with the hurt that we unnecessarily hired an attorney we could hardly afford to work on our case. I informed my attorney of the call, and she said, "Don't worry. I will explain the current situation to her."

"Will this affect anything? Can she sabotage our second

case?"

"No, no. Don't worry. I'll handle it."

I was still worried. I could not explain why.

April 6, 2010, was the day of the interview. It was a nice sunny morning. I dressed the children in adorable outfits, and we brought along some of their favorite toys to keep them occupied. We arrived early. Our attorney had designated a colleague to join us, as she was on a family vacation. He met us in the parking lot, and we went inside the building together.

The immigration building was not the same one we had come to the first time in January 2006. This was new and bigger, and it did not have any of the scents of foreign countries that had filled the walls and ceilings of the older building. After we went through a security detector, we went up to a black man at the front desk and showed him the letter with our appointment time. He was very polite and gave us a number. We took our seats on new shiny chairs and watched the television screens that announced which number was being called next.

The kids had fun playing with other kids in the room, and then our names were called. I looked and saw a white woman in a light-colored business suit.

"That's Officer Green," said our attorney, standing up.

I carried my son and baby bag, and my husband carried my daughter and toys.

"Hello," I said as we approached Officer Green.

She did not respond but merely looked at us loathingly. I wondered if I had imagined her behavior as I set my son on the floor. My daughter sat beside him. They played with the toys, and as each of us took our seats, I noticed that Officer Green was looking at the kids loathingly. She then looked at me with the same level of disdain.

"I don't want your coffee cup on my table," she said.

"Oh, sorry," I said, flustered. "Is there a garbage can I can throw it into?"

"No! I don't want it in my office!"

"I'll take that," said our attorney, and he walked out with the cup.

"Did you bring along credit card bills with both your names on them?" she asked.

We had brought dozens of other financial papers like our income tax papers, house deed, bills, everything. But she had to go and ask for a document that we had not brought along. I began feeling nauseous.

"We've got our credit cards on us," I quickly said. "They have the same numbers."

"Credit cards end in different numbers even if they're from the same account," she said.

"Both of ours end in 3506," I said, and began to look into my purse. "I know the numbers because I pay the bills."

I gave her my card and my husband gave her his. She looked at them unsatisfactorily. Shortly afterward, she said she would review the file and give us a response by the end of the week. We thanked her and walked out, stunned.

"It's okay," said the attorney. "Sometimes they do that. It's not that uncommon."

It was that uncommon, I thought. Normally, unless there was a problem, they gave their approval right there and then.

At home, I crawled into bed and cried my eyes out. I had to interview someone later in the afternoon, the owner of an Iraqi restaurant that was newly opened. I could not get myself out of bed. My husband insisted that I go do the story, said it would get my mind off of things. The night before I had also promised my then potential producer Bonnie I would meet with her after I did the interview with the restaurant owner. I called her to cancel.

"Please, please, Weam!" she begged. "Just for five minutes! It's very important."

"I swear, I'm not feeling good. My head hurts."

"Please, please, please! We can just sit in the car and talk, if you want."

I surrendered, as with Bonnie, it was usually the easier route. She and I later met at the parking lot of a large shopping center. When she saw my van pull in, she jumped out of her orange car and went into my car. She was, as always, dressed sexy, this time in jeans, a tight top that showed a little cleavage, and high heeled shoes. We kissed hello, and she observed my face.

"What's wrong?" she asked. "Did something bad happen?"

"I'm just not feeling well."

"Tell me, please. I'm your friend."

"I can't. Not right now."

"Oh, Weam, my dear sweet sister." She held my hand. "Believe me, whatever your troubles are, just have faith and they will pass. Look at me. I was married to a terrible man, and I told God that if he helped me get a divorce from him, I would have surgery and become a virgin again."

I looked at her in disbelief.

"A lot of people don't know, but I am a virgin, I swear on my daughter's life. Men can't sleep with me. I paid tens of thousands of dollars for this surgery because that was my agreement with God."

I wondered about all her Victoria's Secret emails and hard copy subscriptions. I was in no mood to investigate Bonnie's re-virginity story, but I did wonder if she was telling the truth and whether her sexual stance was why she was unable to close a deal on the movie project.

Bonnie's re-virginity kept my mind off of my troubles during the car ride home. Afterward, reality set back in. Even though my husband and I carried on with my daughter's birthday celebration as if nothing had happened, anytime I was alone, or when no one was looking, tears came down my face.

A month and a half after our interview with Officer Green was when Bonnie set up the lunch meeting at Sahara Restaurant, where I met a man who told me about Dawn Hanna's story. I had gone to the restaurant grudgingly. I was tired of Iraq this and Iraq that and simply wanted to get some fresh air, to take a walk in the neighborhood where I could pick pears and baby green plums off the trees. I went anyway, not knowing that in this meeting I would be introduced to a story that, because of all its heavy political elements, would stretch my literary voice and test my courage. Most importantly, it led me to Lynn Andrews' school.

The day after the meeting at Sahara Restaurant, just after 3 pm, I found in my mailbox a letter from US Department Homeland Security Citizenship and Immigration Services stating that the I-130 petition was approved, but we first had to fill out an I-601 waiver form for grounds of inadmissibility. My attorney called and, with utmost seriousness, asked if we had lied about anything.

"No, everything we told you was true," I said.

"Weam, are you sure?" she asked.

"Yes, I'm sure. I mean, what are they accusing us of lying about?"

"It doesn't say."

"Well, how can we respond to an accusation when we don't know what it is?"

She sighed. "Let me dig into the bottom of this. I'm going to contact the supervisor."

We went back and forth with our attorney and the immigration office supervisor. Officer Green being away on a "training" conference, my husband and I went to the local USCIS office to further inquire about the matter. We were finally told, "Oh, Officer Green made a mistake. She had looked at the wrong file."

Although relieved, I also felt as if I had been played like a rag doll.

Chapter 10
A Fear Doll

I told Fiona that, after years of waiting, we received a letter from Immigration and Naturalization Service regarding my husband's naturalization interview. Not long after that, we received a letter stating that due to unforeseen circumstances, the interview would have to be rescheduled to a later date. The letter did not state when, but said we would be contacted in the near future with further information and that they regretted the inconvenience this may cause. No further explanation was provided, and I knew there was no sense in calling INS for clarification.

I went online and googled whether this type of letter was common. Many posted similar experiences, but no one knew the reasons behind it or how long they had to wait. Some had already waited years. Worry and fear filled those posts. I felt helpless, nervous, and confused.

"Had we not gone through what we went through with INS for the past seven years, I would not be so afraid right now," I said to Fiona after I filled her in on our story. "Over and over again, the government has used different means to terrify us. It's as if we're defending ourselves for simply being born in a certain country. They prolonged our application seven years, interrogated us several times, and harassed us in a way to let us know they have the power to destroy our family. I watched this knowing that it is true. If they decide to do so, I could not stop them from taking away my husband and letting my children be without a father."

I broke down and wept, my whole body shaking at this horrid idea which I had never dared verbalize before.

"I want you to make a doll, a fear doll," she said. "The left side representing fear of the male aspect, of the patriarchal society, which is real, and the right side would be fear of the feminine, which is fear of loss of the family unit. This is to shift energy out of you and into the doll. It doesn't have to be a doll. It could be a coat hanger. It could look like a blob."

I collected myself in order to take notes.

"The more you feed into this fear, the bigger it gets," she said. "If you put that fear and energy into a doll or an object and let it stay there, it will not be on you anymore. Have a basket, and every time that fear comes up, write it on a piece of paper and put that thought on that paper in the basket. What that says is that you are empty enough for new thoughts."

"I've had to deal with so many issues just because I was born in a certain country. I did not choose to be born there. I did not choose to come here. Yet where I was born kept me from moving forward in my career, and it affected my relationship with people I love."

I told her about Chip, my Native American teacher who I loved very much. For my wedding, he gifted me a war painting that conflicted with my beliefs, especially at that time. The US had invaded Iraq a few years prior, causing my family and I great pain. The painting was of a veiled woman holding a baby with tears coming down her face. Behind her, smoke filled the air of burning oil wells. When Chip showed me the painting, I thought it was the ugliest painting I'd ever seen. As he showed me the painting, he said, "This is a woman who's leaving her country behind and walking toward democracy."

I accepted the gift but did not hang it on my walls. This eventually caused him and his female companion, who was also my teacher and who I also loved very much, to cut me off. They disappeared from my life because my political views differed from theirs.

"They ostracized you for having an opinion," Fiona said.

"I've had a hard time writing my book for this reason. Losing people I love over my political views made me feel un-American, or worse, anti-American. This contributed to the fear of speaking out."

"Whatever they thought is not true," she said.

There was a long silence. I calmed down a little and wiped away some tears.

"Do you know where your shaman center is?" she asked.

"In the center."

"But where?"

"I don't know."

"Close your eyes. Move your consciousness. Where did it go?"

"Between my stomach and my heart."

"Do you feel a pulse there? A tightness?"

"Yes."

"Your consciousness is your shaman center, above your navel, under your chest. Practice going there regularly. There, energy moves smoothly and whole solutions change and materialize. Then you won't feed into the drama, the investigation they try to pull you in. Your spirit was food for their egos and bureaucracy and all during the interviews they were putting you in a tailspin. Now, this does not mean that the investigation will stop, but now you are able to move and flow along with it without getting snagged."

"I thought I was over them, but I really wasn't," I said, wiping more tears.

"It was like you were cheating on your diet. Still feeding yourself."

"Yes, the seeds of those fears are still inside."

"If you have watermelon seeds, glue them onto the fear doll," she said. "Each seed is for a fear. Pick up the drum or rattle. Have the drum facing your body and you'll hear where the energy is stuck or blocked. Dance it out."

Seeing how much work she had already done on me, I said, "I've been acting fine, but I really wasn't fine."

"If you notice that you're acting fine, stop, dance, and do drum ceremony because you're acting. You're not being true to you. Deal with what's bothering you, and you become you."

My body felt completely different. I relaxed and thanked her.

"You've now returned to that magnificent you," she said. "The energy of what happened between your teachers has gone out of you and now it can just be a story."

The next day I brought into the house a flat piece of wood from the garage. My kids and I glued seeds on it. We placed watermelon seeds on the left side, pumpkin seeds on the right side, and red seeds in the center. I then did a ceremony. I started the fireplace, burned incense, drummed, and then slowly put the wood in the fire. I watched my fears burn. The smell of roasted seeds permeated the room, releasing me from the political silence that my past teachers placed on me by punishing me for having a *view*.

The energy of the Native American women appeared at the

ceremony. It had been a while since I saw them. They had an ancient look with a modern twist. They were short and plump and bundled in scarves, dresses, shirts, and skirts. Some had braids and others had their hair up in a bandana. When the ceremony ended and I went to return my stones and other fetishes to my bedroom, the women's voices followed me. They said in one voice, "This world is nothing. One day you will be like the dust on this earth."

"Everyone tries to instill fear in us," said Pastor Aaron that Sunday at church. "Our government officials like to strike our hearts with fear. Hollywood tends to turn the nicest things into fearful objects, like dolls. Fear can actually be good or bad. It can be healthy. Kids should be afraid to speak to strangers. Fear of not accomplishing your dream can drive you to fulfill your dreams. But fear can also be a bad thing. Fear can cause people to be people pleasers and focus on temporal things, on things that don't, won't matter in the future – like pleasing a boyfriend or girlfriend and not thinking about the consequences.

"A lot of the disorders that exist in our society are due to stress, fear, and anxiety. When we are confronted with an issue, place God at the forefront of it. Go to Him rather than call a friend, husband, wife, or sibling. When we progress, get over our fear, we are telling our fears that we have courage. Fear does not like to be ignored, and it does not like courage. But if all you do is pray without action that means you're emotionally depending on God to fix the problem. You have to pray and get practical.

"Fear can be contagious. It can be passed from generation to generation. If you grew up in a family that worries about everything, this type of fear and worry will seek the soul of a child and can affect generations until someone stands up and ends the cycle. Don't let fear come in and rob your life and your family's life."

That Sunday there was a full moon, and my husband and I attended a wedding. While we were inside the reception, a windy storm toured the majority of neighborhoods, causing a power outage. At home, we slept with flickering candle lights that radiated the silent rooms. The absence of noise caused me to easily release the vibrations of the outer world and travel within, to find the power animals in each of my chakras, an assignment that I had avoided because, up until now, I simply could not concentrate on it. I explored the animal energies that visited me before falling into a deep, faraway, courageous, and safe sleep.

Chapter 11
PATIENCE, MY DEAR, PATIENCE

Through patience, a certain adventure is born. The inanimate objects in my neighborhood suddenly came alive, and I began to feel like I was part of a fairytale. One day I was pulling my children on a wagon during a stroll when I noticed yellow flowers blooming on three consecutive trees near the road. As I came closer to the trees, I smelt a powerful fragrance. I clipped off a small cluster of the flowers and the heart shaped leaves and wondered out loud, "What type of flower is this?"

"This is a dandelion," my son said.

"No, it's not a dandelion," I said, impressed by his four-year-old vocabulary.

My children wanted to guess what this flower could be, but I was unable to speak because the fumes of someone barbecuing caused me to cough. I continued on home and googled images of "Michigan trees with yellow scented flowers" and I discovered this was a linden flower from a linden tree. Linden trees can live to be a thousand years old, and in Europe, its flowers were used for centuries for herbal teas and herbal medicine to treat a wide range of health problems, even to soothe nerves and anxiety. They are very important honey plants for beekeepers.

"The people that came here cut all the trees because we were using it for medicine," the Red Indian had once said to me. "The trees you see here were planted about two hundred years

ago. None are the original trees. They did not want you to reme-
dy and heal yourself but to need their doctors and hospitals." He
added, "I'm being radical one way, but it's the opposite of their
being radical the other way."

I called my children over to share the information about
the linden tree, but my son started acting up and our fairytale
world cracked. The following morning I was getting a lot of
work done when my son woke up earlier than usual and asked
that I take him to the bookstore right away. Super-duper nicely,
I replied, "Honey, I cannot take you to the bookstore right now,
but in a little bit we can go."

"No, I want to go now!" he cried, and threw a tantrum.

Having a million and one things to do, I tried to avoid him.
The house was a mess, and I was preparing a manuscript for a
poetry contest with today's deadline. But I could not focus on
anything. He remained a few feet from me as he went on about
the bookstore. I reasoned with him, became stern, threatened
to punish him. Nothing worked. I finally broke down crying. I
felt like nothing I did was good enough, and the more I did the
more I was expected to do on my own.

Seeing me break down, he ran into the attached garage and
sat in the van. He kept the door open so I could still hear him
crying even as my crying got louder, deeper. I verbally cussed
out all those who avoided helping me over the years, who ne-
glected to observe my needs and lend a hand. I had always been
there for them. Why was it that when my turn came, they disappeared like an ice cube in water?

When I was done crying, I felt clear and good, as healthy as
an apple. I thanked God for this ceremony, understood the gift
behind the tears and the breakdown. The truth was I somehow
caused my family to not help out much because I wanted to gain

the sort of independence that came along only when faced by a wall. That's when our creative survival mode kicks in. Writers birth books into the world through this type of solitude.

Having taken responsibility for this experience, I calmed down and looked around and noticed that my son was no longer crying. He was still in the car. I went and asked him why he was still there.

"I can't get out," he said sadly. "And I'm hungry."

I rushed to get him out. Carrying him into the kitchen, I kissed and hugged him.

The rest of the day resumed nicely. At my daughter's soccer game, I sat on the grass under the warm sun while my son played next to a tree with one of the other team member's baby sister. They threw sticks at the fence and a small dog behind the fence barked at them. My daughter and the other defense girl twirled their braids as they chit-chatted. The ball came toward them. I called for my daughter to pay attention. Smiling wide, she followed the crowd of girls hovering over the ball, but she did not attempt to tackle it. It was not in her to use any type of aggression unless that aggression was directed toward her brother. I saw myself as a young girl in love with books, not sports. The only person I used to beat up was my younger brother, until he physically outgrew me.

My daughter waved at me. I waved back, cheered her on, and then allowed my gaze to turn to the sun. Once the soccer game ended, I planned to do the water spirit ceremony. I just had not decided where to go yet. Where was there a body of water that I could drum next to without people seeing me and thinking I was crazy?

Her team "Superstars" lost, but my daughter was as happy as could be. She and her brother grabbed the drinks and snacks passed out after the game and we went into the car.

"Where are we going now?" she asked, munching on her chips.

"I have to do something," I said.

We stopped at 7-11 and picked up more snacks and two Slurpees. Then I drove to the pond that once upon a time connected three of the Namou homes on Pond View Drive. This was my brothers' way of making up for that one luxury house that had slipped from my father's hands. Now they had three homes that bent around the same pond. Trees surrounded this manmade pond, where in the summer, ducks gave birth to a new generation of ducklings, and in the winter, the neighborhood kids ice skated or else played hockey. Of the dozen or so homes that surrounded the pond, three belonged to the Namou's. Years later, and one by one, the houses were lost, either to a divorce or by going into foreclosure.

We made a picnic on the grass on a little mound that faced our old home. The area we sat on allowed me to view all three of the Namou homes. My eyes soaked up our surroundings. When this was my neighborhood, I was a single woman waiting to find her perfect man and start a family. I observed my children. They happily walked around the edge of the pond, lightly touching the water and throwing rocks into it.

I picked up the tambourine and made a few soft strikes. I'd bought this tambourine long ago in Sicily, the largest of the Italian islands. In recent years, it had sat in our basement, where my children often played with it. The jingles the metal disks produced would vibrate from the basement all the way upstairs to the kitchen, where I would be cooking a meal or washing dishes.

After the start of the school's second year, I saw it lying near the staircase for several weeks. Finally I picked it up one day and stared at the painting on the skin head. It was of a man and woman dressed in folklore costumes and dancing in unison. They were a perfect reflection of where my husband and I were right now. Our eight-year marriage had survived quite a bit of obstacles, financial and otherwise, but we were able to arrive to a place of understanding. It was because the more I understood and accepted myself, the less I needed from him. And the less I needed these things from him, the easier it was for him to give them.

I decided this would be my drum for now, not the *dumbeg*, which I could buy at any time. They were available at most Arabic stores. Tambourines were more closely related to my background, anyway. They originated in the ancient Middle East and ultimately reached Europe. In ancient Sumer, large-frame drums were used in temple rituals. Small tambourines were played in Mesopotamia, Egypt, and Israel and in Greece and Rome and were used in the cults of the mother goddesses Astarte, Isis, and Cybele. Today they are prominent in Middle Eastern folk music and are also used to accompany recitations of the Quran. The tambourine is mentioned numerous times in the bible. It was used in a way that honors and glorifies the name of God.

As I struck the tambourine with the tips of my fingers, the brass jingles rung into my ears, sucking me into the memories of the past, the ten years when I lived in the house on Pond View. My spirit felt huge, capable of swimming across the surface of water in search of my dreams. I observed the ripples in the water. They floated toward my direction but stopped short, about a quarter away from shore, as though there was a block. Remembering what Lynn said about impatience, I continued to drum. Some time passed, I could not tell how long, before I stood up and stared ahead. The sun's rays relaxed over my children's silhouette, shining attractively like the feathers of a peacock. I called out to the kids, told them we had to leave. My eyes returned to the ripples, now reaching the end of the shore. I took a few steps forward.

"To get into the action, I have to get closer to it," I said, repeating the message I had heard from the water. "Go into your dream. Become it."

In the car, my children asked if we could revisit this pond again.

"Yeah," I mumbled, speechless and feeling very far away. I'm not done here, I thought. I need to return to this place another time because I had not received the full message. I told Fiona about my experience, and simultaneously we suggested I revisit the pond.

"It may have been too much for me all at once," I said. "I may have blocked myself from seeing all I needed to see."

"You felt that," she said. "You didn't think that. That's body-mind. It's so nice to hear you be patient with yourself."

"The other day during yoga I remembered something Leslie had told me about the book. When I fretted about when I'd finish the book, she said, 'It will be done when it's done.' It's funny but the next day, I got quite a bit more writing done than usual. I realized that forcing myself to do more was holding me back. I work so hard from morning until night. I don't waste my time one bit, and yet I continuously drive myself to accomplish more, which actually hinders my productivity. All this time, I've abused myself. I didn't have enough compassion for myself and my work and yet expected others to have compassion for me."

"Wow!" she said.

"Yeah, that's what I thought too. Hearing that word abuse really made me see what I was doing to myself."

"For this week, be in your center and see the story as you are right now, as an observer, like you're watching a movie."

* * *

It turned out that another one of my siblings was liked by the Iraqi president's daughters. Hayfa's younger sister was in the same class as my brother. The teacher chose my brother to escort her to the restroom because after much trial and error, she realized that he was the only one who did not peek through the stall's keyhole. The act of peeking through the stall's keyhole had never crossed my brother's mind. He was just happy to leave the classroom.

My siblings' friendship with the presidents' children was no small affair. It led to an invitation to their maternal uncle's house, which was on the same block in Al Sikek. My sister remembers being served homemade yogurt there. She declined, said she did not like yogurt.

"You don't like yogurt?" the lady said. "Try it and see if you will not like this one."

My sister tried it, and it was the most delicious thing she had tasted. She thought, "This can't be yogurt." Then she realized that yogurt made at her house was not the same as yogurt made by aristocrats. Their yogurt was creamy rich, unlike the one at her home, which was watery. My siblings became friends with the uncle's son, who was also in elementary school. He loved playing with rifles. One day when he went on a hunting trip in Tikrit, he accidentally shot himself.

Hayfa ended up dropping out of school. She could not catch

up. During tests, she kept her paper blank. Once, her mother, who my sister described as very polite, humble, and simple, told my sister, "Try to convince Hayfa to stay in school. It would do her so much good."

My sister had a talk with Hayfa.

"I hate school, and I keep failing," Hayfa told my sister. "Even if I tried for the next ten years, I'd still keep failing."

What Hayfa wanted was to get married and be a housewife. She was an attractive and blossoming young woman with a round face, short hair, and a nice figure. She was older than the other girls, having started school later in life, and she cared less about the curriculum than she did about staring through the window at the officers patrolling the radio station across the street. Hayfa wanted to attain her freedom through marriage. Since she was the president's daughter, her life was closed tightly. A driver took her everywhere, dropping her at the door. She was only allowed to go to school or to relatives' homes, always accompanied by family members or a driver. When the class had a field trip, for instance, her father said she could not go. She decided to go nonetheless by pretending it was a regular school day. The morning of the trip, the teacher wanted to walk down the block to buy oranges. Hayfa asked if she could come along, and when the teacher said yes, Hayfa ecstatically took off her scarf and hurried alongside the teacher.

Hayfa ended up marrying her first cousin General Adnan Khairallah, Saddam's childhood idol, cousin, and his brother-in-law (his wife Sajida's brother). General Khairallah died in 1989 in a helicopter crash during a sandstorm. When announcing Khairallah's death, Saddam referred to him as one of the distinguished war heroes and a sparkling sky in Iraq's sky. A statue was erected in Baghdad in his memory.

Many Iraqi people are certain that Khairallah's popularity within the Army led Saddam to order his assassination. Some say there is no evidence of that, that Saddam actually loved Khairallah very much. The people who Saddam loved and who he suspected were a threat to him were usually assigned a job overseas. Like in the 1968 Baath-led bloodless coup, when President Arif's palace was stormed by four Baathist officers led by Al-Bakr. Arif immediately surrendered and agreed to leave the country. He went to London and then to Istanbul, where he lived in modest obscurity before returning to Iraq some 20 years later. If Saddam did not like the person, that was another story.

"What good did it do us to know the president's daughters?" my brother asked, frowning and throwing the sunflower seed shells he had in his hand into an astray.

Our family was at the park for one of my nephew's birthday, talking about Al Bakr's children and the house we had lost.

"Don't bring up that house," he said, his frown intensifying. "Forget about it."

It was easy to see the hurt and frustration that that house left on my family. And he was right. While my siblings mingled with the Iraqi presidents' children, were even invited to their maternal uncle's house, they were unable to utilize that connection to save the house or to stop the man who had a rift with my father from turning off our electricity, our water, kicking us out of our home, and relocating my father to a faraway city.

Chapter 12
DEALING WITH A CHAMELEON

A cardinal landed on my patio table. His red color brightened up my mind and heart. He jumped on the chair, then on the floor and picked up the seeds left over from when my in-laws were over our house a few days ago. I stopped writing in my journal and looked up his totem. A cardinal's power is year-round and reflects the rhythm of the number twelve: twelve days, twelve weeks, twelve months, or the hour of twelve. When the cardinal flies into your life expect a change to occur within twelve days, twelve weeks, twelve months or at the hour of twelve.

The number of days until Storm Eagle was twelve weeks. I had set my intent, as Fiona suggested, to go to this gathering and meet Lynn in person, my mentors, and the other apprentices, some of whom I had developed a nice relationship with. Storm Eagle was only a four-day trip since I'd planned on skipping registration night. I had gone on four-day trips before. Last year, I went to two four-day writing retreats. My husband was not too supportive of this particular trip, but I hoped he would come around.

I mowed the lawn before dressing the kids and driving to my cousin Angel's house. Four months had passed since we learned that Luke had sold our grandfather's land behind our backs. Luke promised his brother Saul, the mediator, that he would make the situation good by giving us the original deeds. Of course, he postponed the promise like one postpones a visit to the lion's den. He completely lost our trust, so we warned him, through the mediator, that if he made one sly move, we would no longer speak to him or attend any event where he was present. He gave us his word of honor, which for us was as pointless as measuring a bird's testes.

The drama continued, dragging along with it our two remaining paternal aunts, one who lived in California and the other in Australia. One of the cousins in California even buddied up with Luke because she felt this was the diplomatic way to get him to confess pertinent information, such as which of the three lands had he sold and for how much did he sell them. Most importantly, she wanted him to turn over the deeds. Evidently, she had a knack for dealing with thieves.

One day Luke called and said that he had the deeds and he was willing to hand them over to us. We set up the long awaited meeting at his sister's house. We all agreed beforehand that there would be no yelling, no name calling, and no one would hop off of his or her chair like a rabbit. We concluded that we would behave in a civil manner, and I imagined the bourgeois society in movies where people dealt with an insult as calmly as they rubbed a newborn's cheek. I knew the odds of acting civil in a Middle Eastern dispute were a thousand to one, but not wanting to burst anyone's bubble, I played along. To minimize the chances of a brawl, we restricted the meeting to include certain family members who, over the years, had proven to be less likely to lose their temper.

The children happily rushed into the house. Walking into the living room, I avoided Luke's eyes as I said an inaudible hello to everyone. I headed to the kitchen, where my cousin was preparing pasties. I asked if she needed help.

"Could you pour the tea?" she asked. She placed a thick homemade yogurt into a bowl and then arranged honey-filled wafer cookies and meat pies on separate plates.

Angel and I carried the tea and pasties into the living room and set them on the table. Then we sat down. The tension sucked the air out of the room. No one could speak. A few people took their cups of tea, and someone's loud slurp agitated me as I wondered who would start the conversation.

"The deeds arrived earlier this week," Luke said casually, "and I mailed them to our cousin in California."

The slurping stopped with an impact that one experiences when a driver presses on their brakes to prevent an accident. Everyone scanned everyone else as if to ask, "Did he just say what I think he said?"

"Why did you do that?" asked Saul, Luke's brother from another mother.

"I did that because the aunt in California is still alive. As Namou's daughter, she has seniority."

The calm and gentle way in which he spoke, an attribute we highly praised in him in the past, now smelled like cat urine.

Saul jumped to his feet, breaking the agreement that no one was to hop off their chair. He said, "You knew from the start that all of Namou's children, whether alive or deceased with children, have equal rights to the inheritance."

"Exactly," said Luke. "That's my point. They have rights too."

"If we have equal rights, why would you give it to them and not your own brother? This whole summer, I've talked to you two to three times a week. You promised you would bring the deeds and fix the situation between the families. Everyone agreed that I would go to Iraq, hire an attorney in Telkaif to sell the land, and distribute the inheritance properly." He wandered in the small living room, like a sheep without its shepherd. He stopped and looked at Luke. "What am I supposed to do now? Before I go to Iraq, I have to go to California to get the deeds?"

"I can get you the deeds."

"Then why did you send them in the first place?"

"This is going to start World War III," Angel said jokingly.

"This is not funny!" I snapped, and her face turned white and became distorted.

I knew she simply intended to break the ice. Still, it was inappropriate to treat this issue lightly. Her family's attitude toward Luke's wrongdoing had been trivial from the start. Rather than call it by its true nature, an act of deceit, they tried to disguise it by scribbling crayons on top of it.

"Hey, we did not know about any of this," said Peter, acting for once low-key. The tension had hypnotized him. "This is news to us."

"If we were the type, we can get you into a lot of trouble," I said to Luke.

Luke arched one brow and smirked. "What can *you* do?"

He silenced me. He knew that as a cousin, and given how lousy the Iraqi government operated, my threat was as real as a unicorn. A unicorn had more substance than my threat since a creature recently found in southern Europe looked in many ways like the unicorns depicted in medieval tapestries and European folklore. I tried not to lose heart. The world has as many ways to teach someone a lesson as people have ways to lie, cheat, and steal.

"We're done with you," I said. "From now on we will never go where you are. Not even if your sister marries!"

My words created a chilling effect, it seemed. The smirk became gnarled, and his face turned a yellowish green. He looked like lentil soup. It was as if I had spoon fed him the nightshades I had in my backyard, which my Italian neighbor had advised me to remove because they are poisonous, although I'm not sure that she knew what she was talking about since she had also said that my evergreens were not trees. She said they were wild bushes. I did some research and found that evergreens were still trees.

"But that's not fair for everyone else," Angel said. For the first time, her tone and demeanor was serious. We had evidently struck a nerve.

"There are consequences to what people do, dear cousin," my sister said. "Surely your brother does not expect to screw people over and in return receive nothing but an Indian headshake." Then she addressed Luke. "What you did the first time, selling our grandfather's land, was wrong, but this is worse. The first was done out of greed, but this was done out of hate."

"I don't hate anyone," he said.

"Actions speak louder than words," I said.

He stared boldly at me, and I did not recognize his eyes. He had switched into another person. It was like observing a piece of chocolate for a long time and suddenly you notice it is not chocolate at all, but a pet's dung.

Not long ago, everyone thought Luke an angel sent from heaven. He behaved with the grace of a nun, going to church on Sundays, insisting to pray before he ate, and never gossiping or blaspheming. He did not complain, get easily agitated, or raise his voice. He worked as a chef and yet maintained the cleanliness of a nurse. Once when he stopped at his sister's house right after work, I reviewed his crisp white shirt and asked, "Did you change your work clothes before you came here?"

"This is what I wore at the restaurant," he said.

I studied the shirt more closely. It did not have a speck of dirt or stain. "Are you sure you are a chef at the restaurant and not the host?" I joked.

He laughed. "I always dress like this to work," he said in that cool manner of his that could not be fired up even if you lit a match and threw it at him.

"Why did you send the deeds to California?" Angel asked Luke.

"I thought it was the right thing to do," he said.

"That makes sense, since you are such a righteous person," I said. "I'm curious, though. Have you ever met our cousins in California?"

"Once when I was a child they visited Iraq."

"Once when you were a child," I repeated, nodding my head. "So basically, you entrusted the deeds to people you hardly knew rather than give them to any one of your siblings here, like Angel or Saul?"

"I guess I could have done that, but…I tried to talk to you guys. I even called you twice and you did not answer."

"Is that it? You were upset that we did not forgive you overnight? You could not give us a month or so to grasp the idea of you having deceived us for years."

He lowered his head.

"Aside from not answering the phone, did any of us attack or harm you in any way?" I asked. "Call you names? Go around the community spreading the news of what you did?"

"No."

"I cannot believe this," Saul said as he paced in the room. "How could you do this to me? You sending the deeds to someone you barely know instead of giving them to your older brother is like telling me, 'fuck you.'"

"Luke, you said what you did the first time was a mistake," my sister said. "What you did now, what was that? Another mistake?"

He did not respond.

"You are not our cousin," she said. "Right now I don't know who I'm talking to."

"If you give me a chance, I will make things right," he said.

"This was your chance!"

Shortly afterward my sister and Saul said they had to leave. I would have left with them, but it took a while to gather the kids, who complained that they were starving. I fed them spaghetti while I stood in the kitchen with Luke, Angel, and Peter.

"Get the deeds back," Angel said to Luke.

"Yeah, I will," he said.

"I have to go," I said, unable to stand there any longer.

"Yeah, me too," Luke said. He kissed his sister goodbye and then, with much hesitation, leaned over and kissed me on the cheeks. "Don't be upset at me," he said and quickly left.

On my way home, I could not believe how well Luke had camouflaged his deceit through a clean surface. It was like seeing a sparkling kitchen only to open the pantry and refrigerator and find mildew, rats, worms, and ants.

My husband asked me how the meeting went. I told him what had happened and he thought Luke a bastard for playing us like that. Then he told me that his cousin was in Miami right now and he might have gone to Miami with him had it not been for me.

"What are you talking about?" I asked. "I didn't even know about this Miami thing."

"You said you wanted to do a family trip, and so I skipped taking a trip with my cousin. Then you said you couldn't find the right place or the right deal."

"So it's my fault that the family trip didn't work out? I sat for hours on the computer trying to find us a house up North, and everything was booked up until September. And remember when I tried to book for Myrtle Beach? The prices doubled as soon as I went to hit the reserve button."

He chewed his food, pretending like he was not buying my excuses. I was so irritated.

"Anyway, I don't think that it's right to go on vacation with single guys when you're married," I said.

"You went on three vacations last year."

"Those were business trips!"

"What about California?"

"That was years ago, and it was also a business trip and I was miserable the whole time without the kids."

"Still, you've gone to how many places on your own and I've gone to how many places on my own?"

He'd never went on a trip on his own.

"Well, I don't plan on taking any more trips, that's for sure," I said. "Except for the one in the fall, to meet my teachers."

"You're not going."

"What? Why?"

"I'll talk to you about it tomorrow."

"No, I want to talk about it now!"

"I'm tired. I want to go to bed."

"No, because tomorrow will come and you'll say you'll talk to me about it later and later again and we never end up talking about it."

"I can't talk right now."

"Why don't you want me to go on this trip?"

"God willing."

"God willing what?"

"I said, God willing."

"But what does that mean?"

"We will see. Pray God your work will succeed."

"Pray God my work succeeds? So is this about money?"

He ignored the question and again prayed that my work succeeds. I had no energy to argue. I did not want to argue. Since the end of last year my husband and I were meeting eye-to-eye with almost everything. Our relationship had improved to the point where we rarely argued. I loved how far we had come, and I did not want to put a wedge between us, not over a trip. I did want to understand the roots behind this conflict, but not now.

My head pounded at the thought of how much Luke had fooled us. What he did reminded me of the way people, relatives included, took advantage of my father's kindness. I thought about the house that was on the brink of completion but was never completed, of the land deeds that were withheld from my father, of the "financial struggle" gene that was passed onto us, which I did not know how to get rid of or if I would ever get rid of. What he did reminded me of the many times I had gotten close to success, yet each time the opportunity slipped out of my hands and flew away like a bird.

Chapter 13
DEALING WITH SELF

I woke up feeling like a big rock sat on my heart. The game Luke had played on us continued to linger throughout the day, and I could not work properly. It did not help that my husband was against me going to Storm Eagle and my manuscript was not around to distract me. After several revisions, I had turned it over to an editor to critique it, determined that this time, I would get it right. I'd tell an important story in a literary way. The editor said she would have it done in six weeks. During that time, I no longer had a story to wake up to in the morning, to mull over and dress up with the right words and sentences. The absence of my manuscript made me feel a little empty and awkward. Although I quickly replaced these feelings with trips to functions, parks, and the swimming pool, today I could not distract myself whatsoever.

Once my husband came home, I set his dinner on the table and took a walk in the neighborhood. I needed to clear my head and be alone with nature. I marched as if I was dying for air. A Chaldean elderly man and woman in their pajamas were sitting on folding chairs on their front lawn. They watched me curiously. Once I passed them, I pressed my hands against evergreens whose branches burst from the holes of wired fences, like the fat rolls of a woman in a tight dress. I stopped under a huge tree that had what looked like green beans dangling from its branches. I picked up a few of the long seed pods covering the ground to see if they were green beans. They were not. Later I learned this was a catalpa tree.

Thoughts of our past financial struggles continued to agitate me. I passed two men sitting in their open garage playing backgammon and kept treading, waiting to come across the two pear trees that, like sisters, were side by side, reachable to the hands of a passersby. One had green baby pears, the other red baby pears. I always reached out and picked a fruit, rubbed it against my clothes, and ate it as I walked, at the end throwing the core for the squirrels and other creatures that also delighted in its taste. Other surrounding trees had apples, peaches, and baby green plums, but a fence prevented people from plucking them off.

I reached the video store at the corner of the main streets without seeing any of the fruit trees I had anticipated. On the way back, I kept an eye out for the pear trees, not because I was hungry and needed the fruit for nourishment or because their taste was irresistible and could not be matched by the ones sold in the produce market. I loved the joy, freedom, and spontaneity this simple act provided. So many walls and borders were placed between us and nature that sometimes it felt like we were living in a zoo.

I could not spot the trees anywhere and was confused. Suddenly a squirrel ran beside me on top of a fence. He behaved as if he was racing me. He won and I laughed, not just at the squirrel's behavior but at the absurdity of this whole land inheritance. It seemed so little in the big scheme of things. "It's no big deal," I told myself and remembered what my sister had said to me when she called that morning.

"Don't be bothered by what Luke did," she said. "We might

not be able to take legal action, but in this world, there are three types of laws. The first is legal law, the second is tribal law, and the third is God's law. So if he is not punished by the legal system, he still has to suffer the consequences the tribe will place on him. And what God will do – that's another story. That's the ultimate punishment."

I decided to leave this issue to God and focus on how forcing myself to do more was holding me back. How could I heal that part of me because, as Lynn said, we are the only ones who can heal ourselves? Oh, if only I could go see her at Storm Eagle! Why was my husband against me going? Would it make a difference if I was using my own money? I had put whatever I had into editing the manuscript. I had nothing left, not even money to cover the school tuition. I shared my thoughts with one of my nieces, one of three who I was a godmother to. We were driving home after eating dinner at another niece's house. It was a good forty-five minute drive, and, what with her being a good listener, I knew that I would arrive to my answer by the time we arrived home.

"Do you know why he does not want you to go on this trip?" my niece asked.

"First, it bothers him that I took three trips last year when he took zero. I explained those were business trips but to him they provided the type of rest that he has not had in a long time. Second, I had tried to plan a family vacation since last September and always, for one reason or another, it just hasn't worked out so I decided to stop. Third, for nearly two years now I have not brought in income – especially since last year, when I decided to no longer do freelance work. So I don't have the financial independence to push for this. I'd even thought of getting a job or something to get me to Storm Eagle but later realized that was very unrealistic. Freelance writing assignments take months to acquire and, with other types of jobs, I'd need a babysitter. Not enough time to find a job. Only enough time for a miracle."

We were quiet momentarily.

"I need to make a phone call." I called Baghdad Restaurant to order dinner for my husband. A woman answered and said they were closed. Then I called Ali Baba, knowing they stayed open until the middle of the night. He said the food would be ready in twenty minutes.

I hung up the phone and continued. "My concern is that given how old Lynn is, she may die before I can meet her. Aside from that, I want to meet my mentors and experience whatever I'm supposed to experience at Storm Eagle. At the same time, if I don't have my husband's support when he'd be the one who would watch the kids, I don't feel I can fight for this. I don't have the energy. And it would defeat the purpose – enjoying the trip."

"What does your gut tell you?" my niece asked.

I thought of my mentors asking that same question.

"Don't think," she said. "Just answer. What does your gut tell you?"

She sounded just like Leslie and Fiona.

"I feel I could do without the trip," I said. "My mentors said that whatever happens at Storm Eagle quickens our teaching. That may be true, probably is true, although I do believe we should depend on ourselves and God for that. My relationship with my husband has been so good this year I don't want to bring tension to our marriage. I'm very happy where we're at right now. We went from butting heads to becoming a team."

"Mamma, my tummy hurts," my son said.

I reached my hand behind my seat and touched his shoes. "We're almost home, Mommy." I returned to my niece. "Eventually I will meet everyone in person. Next year, for instance, I will be at a much better place career-wise. The kids will be older and..."

I heard my son cough loudly.

"Mom, he threw up on the iPad!" my daughter said.

Flustered, I ran a red light. I realized what I did and panicked. "Oh my God!"

"It's okay, just calm down and keep going," my niece said.

I took a few breaths, thinking how I could have killed us had it not been so late and there was no incoming traffic. At home, as I gave my son a bath, I felt content with the decision not to go to Storm Eagle. Passing a red light signaled that I ought to refocus on my home. I knew that this choice had origins older than the pyramids. Some Eastern family beliefs are difficult to explain in words but easier through a story, like the following story.

David is an American man who once worked as a warden at the US Embassy in Bahrain. The day he arrived to Bahrain International Airport, he learned that contrary to what he had grown up thinking, women in the Arab world do have rights – not as many rights as they need to have, but they do have rights. He was standing in line at customs when a woman just zoomed in front of all the men in line. He called out on her inappropriateness with a "Hey, hey, back of the line!" and suddenly he was surrounded by police and angry civilian men. He knew he'd done something wrong but given the language barriers he couldn't figure out what it was. Seeing what had happened, a British man intervened, explaining to the police that this American did not know the customs of this country, which was that women are allowed to cut in line whenever or however they pleased and no one could say a word about it.

"You don't do what you just did with the women here," the British man said to David.

For the remainder of his stay in Bahrain, David did not dare open his mouth when he begrudgingly watched women cut in line at supermarkets, even when he and other men would have one or two items and the women had ten, oftentimes more. This right may seem like no big deal but to some women, getting to the market and back in time to have a fresh delicious meal prepared for their family is more important than the right to vote for complete strangers.

The next day I stayed home and, for most of the day, transcribed my handwritten journals into Word documents in preparation for my next book, which would be a memoir series about my four-year shamanic school. The editor still had my manuscript, and I thought it would be a good idea to start on my next story rather than sit around counting the number of squirrels, birds, and cats who regularly visited my backyard. The kids kept interrupting me by asking, "Where are we going today?"

"Nowhere!"

A few minutes later I heard them jumping on the bed with the TV so loud I could not think. Something happened because my son started crying, but not the type of dangerous cry where I had to get off my chair and check on him. I heard my daughter say, "Sorry," but he kept crying.

"I said sorry!" she shouted.

"And it still hurts," he yelled.

"Well, it doesn't matter," she said, and they went on playing together. I kept typing away until I heard a big boom. They ran into the kitchen, and I rushed to see what had happened. They were okay, but the drapery in my son's room now lay on the floor. Furious, I told them they were grounded from the TV, iPad, iPhone, iPod, for a week.

"What's a week?" my son asked.

"Twenty-four seven," my daughter said.

"How about for four weeks?" my son asked.

"No, that's even longer," she said.

"Two weeks?" he asked.

"No, that's still longer."

"Don't worry how long it is!" I said, resembling an animal in disguise with my mismatched clothes, socks hanging loose from my feet, my messy hair, and my growling voice. "When it's over, I'll let you know."

I told them to go to their rooms, took their iPad, and surfed Netflix. Figuring that transcribing my journals while watching a movie would make the process more tolerable, I came across a two-part documentary about Woody Allen, which kept me hooked. One statement Woody Allen made resonated so much truth that it erased much of my doubts about directing. He said, "It's not rocket science. This is not quantum physics. If you are the writer of the story, you know what you want the audience to see because you've written it. It's just storytelling, and you tell it. There's no big deal to it."

This made perfect sense. I felt and thought the same way, but the way people responded to my wanting to make films – they looked at me as if I wanted to perform open heart surgery – caused me to have doubts. His words freed me and stirred many desires and emotions. I badly wanted to be in his shoes, and I was afraid that maybe I never will be. Certain days I saw myself constantly standing in the same place, spinning my wheels and moving very little.

The cardinal landed on the patio table. His bright red color in the midst of the greenery made me smile. He flew to the patio chair and jumped to the patio fence then he flew away. I sighed heavily. I wondered if he was trying to tell me anything. The phone rang.

"Could you pick up Mom today?" my sister asked. My mother had temporarily moved into my sister's house because her health had worsened and she needed twenty-four hour supervision.

"Sure. I'll be there in a little bit."

I parked in my sister's driveway. It started raining. I noticed their apple tree looked pretty healthy. Last year black holes filled the core of the baby green apples. So I rushed to the tree, picked four apples, and hurried back into the car. My niece helped my mom walk out from the garage, and she offered to wash the apples I picked.

"You don't need to do that," I said.

My brother-in-law came out with a plastic bag and filled it with apples.

"You don't have to do that!" I said.

"That's okay," he said calmly.

"It's raining! You can gather some for me another day."

By now, the bag was full. He walked toward the car and handed me the bag of apples. "This year the apples are nice and plenty because I sprayed them," he said. "Next year, you might not see any apples."

"Why?"

"Fruit trees that bear a heavy crop one year might not flower the next year."

"Oh," I said, understanding the reason behind the missing pears in the pear trees.

At home, after we settled down, one of my sisters came over to see my mom.

"I like living with your aunt and her husband," my mom said. "They are very good to me."

My sister and I looked at each other, astounded. What was happening to my mother? Why did she forget things easily or often mix up names? To lighten things up, my sister turned what my mother said into a joke and then the phone rang. My brother-in-law asked if he could drop off his mom to my house as she and his wife had gotten into a fight and his mom threatened to run away. I asked what started the fight, and he said that his wife had accused his mother of feeding the dog potato chips, which caused him to throw up.

"Mom, how do you say Burger King in Arabic?" my son asked me as I tried to figure out what to answer my brother-in-law.

My mind buzzed with the chaos. I could barely get my head around it when the sister who my mom lived with said, "I'm ready to switch Mom to another home, if it's available."

Find a home for mom was added to my to-do-list, and later that week, I went with my brother-in-law to the Iraqi Consulate in Southfield. We told them what my cousin had done and asked whether we could reclaim the stolen land or at least safeguard the rest of the lands.

One of the men behind the window reviewed our files and said, "Regardless of whether you have copies of the deeds or the originals, neither your family nor any other family could sell the rest of the land without first getting everyone's consent. The legal procedures are strict, very strict and complicated, since after the war a lot of people were selling land fraudulently. You will need to hire an attorney in Telkaif. I can refer you to this one guy that many people have hired for land issues."

"So the people who have the original deeds have no more or less power than we do?" I asked.

"True."

"Wow, Luke and the Californians screwed themselves over for nothing," my cousin said. "What about the land that was sold fraudulently? Can we do anything to get that back, or can we press charges?"

"You might be able to get the land back, but it's a long process," he said. "You would have to write a report and send it to the police in the province of Mosul. They would then investigate and go from there."

He excused himself for a moment, during which time the other man behind the window who had a shaved head and a red left eye, said, knowingly, conspiratorially, "There are other ways to make him give you the deeds."

We nodded then walked out of the consulate, happy that toilet paper was more useful than the original deeds, but quite disappointed that the land that was sold was gone. Saul went on a mission, telling anyone he came across what his brother had done. The barber, the clerk at the producer market, the diners at the Iraqi restaurants, the home improvement guy, whoever. They told him that they'd heard many stories of relatives stealing and selling land after the 2003 US-led invasion but that this one topped the cake.

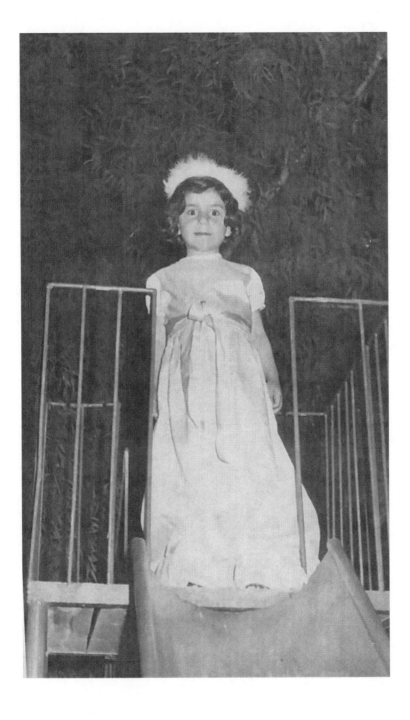

Chapter 14
BORN INTO LUXURY

As I waited for Lynn to come on the conference call, I sat on the living room rug, sorted out mail, and tore up old coupons. She soon entered the call, greeted everyone, and then asked us to take a deep breath and imagine the first sunrise that we ever saw in our life, as a baby. She said, "As you see the sunrise, breathe deeply, and you will see the different coloring around you, the gorgeous shafts of light, the pure gold. Feel what it's like to watch the sunrise in your young silence with the idea that you're going to remember this forever."

She gave us a moment to do that, and I thought about her voice. It sounded thousands of years old, as if it had come from another planet simply to give us a message and depart. She said a prayer, and soon the moderator began to read the questions. I placed the stack of coupons on the floor and grabbed my pen and notebook. The first question came from an apprentice in Germany. She wanted to know how dreaming and attention related to each other. Lynn explained that dreaming was something you want to have alongside freedom, innocence, and perfection.

Lynn said, "If you are shearing through the veils of ignorance, which clump down over your vision through addictions, then you cannot find your dreams. If you come out of any kind of abuse, any reason in life where you're living someone else's dreams, you can't find your own dream. Maybe you can't find your dreams because your parents never allowed it and you were always hiding from them to try to please them. You never understood what it was like to please yourself."

The same apprentice expressed how she noticed that she committed much more to practicing her viola and piano regularly because she met with her teacher once a week and therefore felt obliged to practice. Yet with the school work, things like the shaman dance of power, the shaman breath, yoga or Thai Chi, she was not as dedicated. She wanted to know how she could strengthen her inner teacher so that she could practice equally seriously.

The moderator asked her, "What's the difference between what your music teacher is asking of you and what Lynn Andrews is asking of you?"

"I think there's a *puella* part in me that feels obligated to go back to the teacher and when I go and see him, I really want to be good. I feel guilty if I haven't practiced."

We read about *puellas* in Marie-Louise von Franz's book, *Puer Aeternus*. *Puer aeternus* is a Latin term that means "eternal boy". Franz is a Jungian analyst who gave lectures at the C.G. Jung Institute in Zurich. She describes the man who is identified with the *puer aeternus* archetype as "the man that remains too long in adolescent psychology." It is the Peter Pan syndrome, which was attributed to most notably, Michael Jackson. When the subject is a female, the Latin term is *puella aeterna*. A *puella* is vivacious and child-like, can brighten up a room. But she has difficulty taking herself seriously because she identifies as a girl, not as a woman. She also has a father-daughter relationship wound.

"So with Lynn, in the shaman work, it is giving you much

more freedom to make the choice, and it's a more adult choice," the moderator said. "It's not the *puella's* choice, right?"

"Not only that," Lynn added. "But if you're choosing to practice your music, don't do it because someone is going to be upset with you. Do it because you love it and it is part of the harmony of the universe. You have to learn how to make that music part of the harmony of your own soul. And that's what you're learning in the school."

The next question came from a caller in Spain. She had easily seen her hands in her dreams. They were full of radiant lights of energy because she taught and helped others, but she was having difficulty seeing her feet. Lynn said that happened with a lot of people, and it could be due to having to look down at our feet. She encouraged the apprentice to keep trying, because when one finds resistance, one has to overcome it. She compared it to someone being able to lift weights but not being able to do pushups.

"It's just a muscle, and you're exercising it so you will have control over it. It does not have control over you," Lynn said. "On the other hand, it's not a trying process. Just allow it to happen." She added that she had met a monk in Tibet near the Crystal Monastery who healed and communicated with his feet, even though he had a voice. "When he wants to work on you, he puts his feet on you," she said. "There's as much power in your feet as anywhere else in your body because all of your nerve endings are in your feet."

My daughter barged into the kitchen and asked if she could make a peanut butter and jelly sandwich, startling me. I said she could and asked her to make one for her brother as I carried my coffee cup and notebook to the bedroom, away from the noise. One apprentice said that she did not get symbols when she meditated, and she was quite content to leave everything a blank canvas. Although she was open to receiving symbols, her love and preference was for the blankness. Her concern was whether that would be an impediment to her in any way. The only symbol she received was in a dream, where she was told she could not have symbols.

"Well, that's a symbol," Lynn said. "That in itself is a symbol. What you're discovering is that the most important thing is the unknown. And that is a nothingness symbol. There are a lot of different ways to see symbols. First of all, symbols are without words so that they can encompass a much greater meaning. So I think it's the unknown that's challenging you."

She recommended that the apprentice read and study Jung for a bit. He wrote a book about symbols and meanings of symbols.

"I don't think someone else should interpret your symbols," Lynn added. "Psychiatry is really a very young science, and they have all the symbolism for everything and I think that's incredibly incorrect because everybody has their own symbols from their own experience, which is vastly different from every other person that has ever been born.

"There's so many ways of moving into the unknown, the abstract, the mystery of life, and it's something that we're losing in our society. That's the importance about Twisted Hair, the storytellers. The storytellers would come from other villagers and they would talk about the history and what's happening from other villagers, things that had been learned from the great spirits and the new ceremonies that someone else might be doing. This is how Twisted Hair brought people together in a sacred way. We're losing all of that because of technology and so many other things. But we are going back to that in a way. The ancient knowledge that was taught to us centuries and centuries ago is being remembered and brought back. And that's what we do, help people go back to their original nature.

"You are beginning to remember why you are here in the first place, why you are born. Life is not about rules and laws and belief structures. You were not born to be a lawyer. You were born to be an enlightened being and to be incredibly happy, joyous, and free. That's where the abstract, where the fun is."

The next question came from a woman in Argentina. She wanted to know, "If sound can change and affect the molecules, can the sound from our drums and rattles activate the physical and also perhaps allow us to become young again?"

"Of course it can," Lynn said. "But you have to learn how to regenerate yourself. Let me give you an example. There is an over-soul to this world right now that is very negative. It's a darkness that is resulting in war, chaos, and fear and huge changes and challenges. It's this other force that in a way is the death dance to the patriarch. We're in a great war, a spiritual war. That over-soul of negativity that surrounds us needs food to exist. It's dark. It's vicious, and the more you feed it, the worse it's getting. There are wars now and hatred and so much violence that it's just eating big steaks every night.

"If you could, each time you move into fear or anger or worry or jealousy or any of the negative aspects of human nature, say, okay, I'm going to change this. I'm going to look at my fear and I'm going to say, what needs to be changed? Is there something that I need to pay attention to? If there is, then for God's sake, do it. Do it immediately. Don't wait a day! And if you can't do anything about it, if it's a vague fear that you can't put your finger on, like you might think – oh, my God, what's going to happen when I'm old? You change that fear into a delight that you are alive now! Fill yourself with light. Do not allow yourself to be controlled by a negative force that doesn't belong to you. It's making a slave out of everybody. Everyone is feeling chaos and fear and worry, and it's going to destroy you if you don't stop it. If you can feel love and open your heart to the sense of peace and well-being, you will starve that over-soul to death and it will go away and certainly stop bothering you."

My son opened the door, ran to my bed, and hugged me. He asked, "Mom, is mook healsy?"

"Yes, milk is healthy," I said and tried to shush him.

"Can you put me gween chips and mook?"

"Okay, go." I shooed him out and returned to my call. Lynn was saying, "You might look at this and say, oh my God, what can I do? I'm only one person. You can take care of yourself, be responsible for yourself before you can be responsible to deal at all with anyone else. Shamanism sounds like something very selfish, but it is not. There's absolutely nothing you can do to be a light for anyone else unless you shine that light yourself." Laughing, she said, "I don't remember what the question was."

The moderator repeated the question. Lynn then talked about how the use of drums and rattles can take a person into a place where they can literally reconstitute themselves. They can change their vibrational frequency by moving their consciousness away from depression, for instance. This reminded me when I went through depression. What got me through it was entirely removing myself from my environment and going into environments my soul was drawn to at that time, Europe. The process took me out of my routine and electric shocked the negative thoughts and emotions that I could not otherwise get rid of on my own. The foreign foods, language and people I was introduced to were like a paintbrush that stroked its bristles from my head to my toe, splashing over me brand new colors. By the time I returned home, my mind carried a fresh coat of ideas.

"This next question is from Weam," I heard the moderator say, after I had left for a while to days long gone. "Weam writes, 'I sometimes find myself so intrigued with the school work that I don't want to deal with the outside world. The work takes me to a place of when I was a child – happy, peaceful, and with my-self. Now as an adult, should I oblige to this resistance I have to the outer world or should I work to overcome it?'"

"I so understand how you feel! Oh, boy!" Lynn said. "Re-member when I was in Manitoba with the ladies, my teachers, and I never wanted to go home, I just wanted to stay with them and learn and learn and have fun. To me, that's fun. It's the best fun in the world. And I said, 'Can I stay?' Agnes was incredibly firm with me, packed my suitcase, and said, 'Here! You're leav-ing tomorrow!' I asked, 'Where am I going?' 'You're going to New York.' 'I don't want to go to New York!' 'Yes, you're going to go to New York and you will see your agent. Then you're going to sit somewhere on Madison Avenue and you're going to think about how spiritual you really are. It's easy to be spiritual when you're sitting on the porch or doing ceremony. How easy is it when you are surrounded by traffic and honking and people?'"

Lynn finished the story and paused. Then she said to me, "You need to learn to walk with a foot in the world of spirit and a foot in the world of the everyday. You were born in a land that speaks English, mostly, and you speak English because it is a materialistic language, meaning it's a pragmatic language. It's about survival, it's about living in the world, in the physicality of the world, and you need to understand that. It's part of your learning. It's very difficult, and I know you want to stay here, but you can stay here in your heart. You have to be able to move in both worlds equally."

Her story so resembled mine, I wished to be able to see her in autumn at Storm Eagle, to have conversations with her in person, to experience her on a closer level.

"I know how hard it is," Lynn said to me, laughing. "But you have to be able to do both. Does that help at all?"

"That does help. I spent a lot of time over the weekend on the school work, went really deep into it. Then Monday came and it was all about taking the kids here and there. I was having a harder time than usual doing the basic necessities because in the back of my mind, I just wanted to get back to that place of mysticism. Sometimes I wonder, what is the point of dealing with the outside world?"

"I understand and you know, love yourself for it. Maybe you just need to allow yourself to let it be a cocoon of beauty around you for a while. The school is a wonderful experience, and I don't think it would hurt you at all to do that for a while, to remain in the school work."

"That's what I want to do. I want to give myself that permission. On one hand it might seem selfish, but I want to go ahead and give myself permission to take more time."

"But enjoy it! Don't feel guilty about it. You know everything we've talked about tonight is about allowing yourself to do all of the things that we talked about. Just allow; open your heart. For heaven's sake, if you're not having any fun and enjoying it and loving yourself, then you're doing something wrong."

"Thank you," I said.

The moderator said she would go a little faster because only five minutes were left. She read a question from a woman in Spain. "Lynn, you've always told us that what we imagine is real.

I want to ask you what is the difference between what we see in visions and ceremonies and what we see in magical thinking."

"What you imagine is true because take a look at your body," Lynn said. "That's what you imagined. You have created this. You have created your life. Look around you. If there is something you are not happy with, why have you created that? Why did you need to learn that lesson, whatever it is? You said something else, but I lost it here."

"What's the difference between visions and ceremonies and magical thinking?"

"What you imagine is magical thinking. You know, you worked with your imagination. It's a muscle, like anything else. Those synapse connections have to fire, and you have to teach them to fire because if you don't work on them, they start to go dormant. So what you imagine is real, but it may be more powerful when you are using those synapse connections.

"Your body is constantly reforming. Every seven years, you have a new cellular structure. So you are responsible for your life, and if you don't like what you see, then change it, whatever it is. Magical thinking…you cannot have magic in your life if you do not believe in magic. What is magic? It's the unknowable. It's that wonderful aspect of the unknowable where things happen that you can't even imagine, where you'll be thinking of an old love that you had not seen in thirty years and you turn a corner and there he is in a place that you can't imagine. That's magic. That's the mystery coming to you and being present."

"Magic is beyond the imagination," the moderator said. "It's where imagination meets mystery."

"Yes, it's where imagination meets mystery," Lynn said.

I badly wanted to meet Lynn in person. After each call, my

yearning for her teachings grew more and more. Her answers to the apprentices' questions were so constructive that they seemed to serve everyone on the call. It would be great if the teachings were more intimate and received in person. I shared my feelings with Fiona during our next call.

"Lynn teaches great teachings that come from the feminine," Fiona said. "No power struggle, like when there's a male figure. When you're with her, you know that Lynn is powerful and can stand in her power and she'll never let you feel below her unless you allow her to feel more powerful. And then that's not what it is really."

I understood. Lynn did that with me last year during a phone session when she saw my hesitation about going to the writer's retreat. The mirror she held up ignited a potent force within me, revealing the fears and the self-worth issues I had hidden in the dark basement. She woke up my senses so I could stop tiptoeing around my dream and dive in. If over the phone she could shift my energy the way she did and offer me a new viewpoint, how much more effective would her work be in person?

"When I'd first spoken to Lynn, it was my first encounter of knowing unconditional love," Fiona said.

I went to bed that night thinking that maybe, just maybe, I would still go to Storm Eagle and be blessed by Lynn's love and work. Miracles happen overnight, and there were many nights between now and autumn. Fiona connected me to a woman who used to be a mentor for Lynn's apprentices. She had also helped put together the study guide for Lynn's Writing School. She now paints. She lived in Michigan but had a home close to Lynn's in Arizona and was very close to Lynn. I told her my issues with Storm Eagle, the conflict of whether I need to push to attend the gathering or just let it be.

"Storm Eagle is very important," she said. "It allows you to see your mentors and classmates. Because you're in a Mystery School, subtle energies are afloat and they almost float underground. First year is cool. Second year your eyes open, and when your eyes open everything else opens. This is not a cult. It's a wonderful place to experience things. And when the four to five days are over, it feels like you finished a great big book. And you think to yourself, 'I'll never be the same after reading the book.'"

I sat outside on the porch, taking notes and reflecting on her words.

"Being at Storm Eagle is like being Alice in Wonderland," she said. "You get a whole lot of information, you feel very much alive, and you basically, at the core, stay the same. Going to Storm Eagle is like saying I'm worth it. You're marrying yourself."

"My agent said that this one producer likes my script. He's in LA. I was hoping that, if there's real interest, I could use this as an excuse, or push, to go."

"Women are like that," she said sadly. "We have to have an excuse to do what we want. It's like we're speaking in slow motion. It's hard not to do that because then you're taking responsibility for your happiness. You can't blame it on your husband, on your kids, on your mom – no one."

I was quiet.

"I can tell you're hungry, hungry for you," she said. Later she told me that not long ago she had taken a rest from some of the work with the school. "I was so involved in everything that I was just like this banquet table."

Ironically, this had the strongest meaning for me. With two

young children, no nanny or full-time babysitter, the book to complete, the school work to do, a home to look after, a husband to care for, squeezing one more thing when it was something that was not coming easily felt like I was leaking my energy. I had to finish my book and attain my act of power. I had finished writing it, but I still had a long way to go before the book was really finished. The words "The End" did not constitute a finished book. It was simply as if I had finished sewing an ordinary dress without a touch of adornment. For the dress to be exquisite, couture, I had to invest my heart and soul into the final details. The beads and sequins and stones, the perfection of the hem and zipper, had to be incorporated; they finalized the heart of the dress so it could truly spread love and self-worth to the woman who wore it.

This quote came to mind from Lynn's book, *Jaguar Woman*, when Agnes Whistling Elk said, "Everything you need is here. The things you need are always here; you need to be smart enough to find them."

That week, when I reviewed my second quarter task sheet to turn it in to my mentor, I discovered I had somehow missed an assignment. We were to meditate with four different partners who were near or far in distance. During the meditation, we had to reach the point where our partner's power animal could say something like, "I really need help with this being that I work with because she lacks discipline" or "He needs to make more acts of power, create more mirrors for himself." We were to listen to whatever the other person's power animal discussed with us and then share it with our partner.

First I partnered with the woman from Colorado, who'd had coffee with me at the airport last year. Her power animal was the finned whale. She told me that the finned whale was the second largest whale in the world. It does not have teeth, so they eat shrimp and such. They swim very deep and they are not competitive.

After our meditation was over, we called each other.

"The wolf says you need to stop doing so many different things so you can do whatever you do well," she said. "He says that family is the most important to take care of. He wants you to not move. You need to make tools to help you get out of your head so much. There is no right or wrong answers. The wolf says to tell you that you are doing very well, but you make yourself suffer because you always feel like it's not good enough. Always someone needs something from you. You need to allocate more of the chores throughout the family. You need self-time so you can be more present and enjoy your family more."

After I shared the message her power animal had for her, we hung up and I sat still on the patio deck, staring at the evergreens. My children played on the swing set, their chatter trailing through the air and drifting into an echo in the sky. A robin landed on the red barbecue grill that was a Father's Day gift for my husband a few years back. I took a deep breath and thought of the ways I'd squandered my time doing this and that for others. Sometimes it did not look like I was doing it for them, or at least I tried to convince myself of that. But it was for *them* and none of it held any real substance. For one month, while the manuscript was out of my hand, I was free to do whatever pleased me, but I ended up submitting to the needs of two women who had marital issues that only God could resolve, if even. I thought I was doing a good thing when really I simply had not mastered the art of graciously saying, "No, thank you."

Two red birds landed together on my patio table. One of

them was the usual guy who visited. He had a bright, deep red plumage and a black face. The other one, the female, was dull red with reddish tints on the wings and tail feathers. The phone rang, interrupting my admiration for these little creatures. It was my sister. I told her I would call her back, and by the time I hung up, the red birds had flown away. I went outside with my journal and sat to write. Since I wanted silence, I did not call my sister back. I'd already spent the morning with enough phone calls – updates about what our cousins were saying about the godforsaken land, a friend had personal issues, and finally, the meditation with the power animals, where I realized I must stop this noise.

A plane passed by. A baby bee landed on my journal, its wings colorful with the sun rays. The bee is a reminder that activities are more productive and sweeter if we take time to enjoy them. It reminds us to extract the honey of life and to make our lives fertile while the sun shines. Bees are the symbol of fertility and sexuality, of accomplishing the impossible. Aerodynamically, its body is too large for its wings and it should not be able to fly. Although people now understand how it flies, high rate of wing movement, the bee remains a symbol of accomplishing anything we put our mind to.

The second person I partnered with was from Spain, a woman I had never spoken to before. We met at 5 pm my time, midnight her time. Her power animal was the eagle. We meditated and then emailed each other with what we saw. She saw a fully grown black wolf, most likely a male wolf. She wrote, "The way I felt it, you have a very old soul with much wisdom that is waiting to be self-discovered and you need to awaken that wisdom to be able to share with others. I asked the wolf if he had any messages for you, and he told me you are a strong woman even if at times you don't feel it. Also sometimes doubt stalks you regarding your role as a mother. You ask yourself, am I a good mum? Am I doing things right? The wolf told me you are a wonderful and caring mother and that you are doing a marvelous job. I was shown an image of a beaver. I asked why, and he told me that is how you are. You work hard in every way, with work and family. You always want the best for everyone, and you want everyone to be happy."

My eyes were glued to the computer screen. I could not believe the accuracy of her description, especially since I had never spoken to this woman before. How was she able to know? Did my power animal, the wolf, really exist? My first-year mentor helped me meet him, and I have talked to him here and there and made efforts to have a relationship with him, but I viewed him somewhat as an invisible friend, another way of communicating with my subconscious mind. Was I underestimating the power of a power animal?

I continued to read. "The wolf also told me to tell you to always stay strong and to be ready for any battle as at times situations affect you a lot. I was then shown a sacred palace in India with an enormous path that ended at the entrance of the palace. The wolf told me, 'She sometimes sees her spirituality very far and difficult to achieve, making her path even longer to reach. Tell her she will know when she is ready.' I asked him, ready for what? And he answered, 'She will know.'"

Goose bumps rained over me. Fiona said earlier this year that goose bumps are from memory. She'd said, "Your physical body is a vibration of yourself remembering who you are without stories."

I reread the part about India and remembered that the

night before I had grabbed off my bookshelf *Daughter of Fire: A Diary of a Spiritual Training with a Sufi Master*. This was an 820-page book which Narendra, my spiritual teacher from India, suggested I read some twenty years ago. The diary spans five years and it is about Irina Tweedie, a British woman transformed at the hands of a Sufi Master in India. Tweedie is the first Western woman to be trained in this ancient yogic lineage. When I first read this book, I immediately reread it. Years later, I read it again. I wished I could read it now, but 820 pages for me these days was like trying to climb Mount Everest.

I flipped through the pages and came across a passage about how those that are able to let themselves go, who know how to lose themselves, can go further spiritually than intellectuals. I flipped through more passages and noticed how differently I viewed the messages today than I did twenty years ago.

*She sometimes sees her spirituality very far and difficult to achieve, making her path even longer to reach...*I must ease up on myself, mustn't I? A yoga teacher once said to us, "Calm the mind. You will go further." Suddenly, I thought about all my spiritual teachers and how involved I have been in this work since my early twenties, almost as involved as I am with my writing. They actually went hand-in-hand.

You have a very old soul with much wisdom that is waiting to be self-discovered and you need to awaken that wisdom to be able to share with others. The Spanish woman's words replayed in my head like a recording. The words had the gentleness of singing birds but were as powerful and loud as thunder. By sharing my teachings with others through my writing, I would be helping, and by helping, the circle of my writing career would be complete. The question then was, how far or close was I to completing that circle? How could I shed off the issues of lack of self-worth and arrive to the time and place of my birth?

I was born into luxury, in the house which my siblings refer to with nostalgia as *beit Al Sikek*, the house of *Al Sikek*. It was right around the time my father received free land from the government to build a home on. My mother's water broke one winter day in December, and she told my fifteen-year-old sister Niran to go call the midwife. Niran rushed to the neighbors to use their phone. The midwife was not home so Niran left a message that my mother was in labor. Niran and Awatif, another sister who was thirteen years old, then nervously paced the front of the house, waiting to get a glimpse of the midwife. They saw my great-uncle's wife, Hannia, walk up with her son.

"What's the matter with you girls?" she asked.

"Our mother is in labor," they said.

Aunt Hannia immediately pushed through the front doors, removed her veil, and ordered my sister to boil water. She went into the room where my mom laid. My sister brought the boiling water, and then Aunt Hannia ordered them out of the room.

"If it's a boy, you can keep him," my great-aunt said to my mother. "If it's a girl, I'll reserve her for my youngest son." Her youngest son was barely out of diapers at that time.

Within half an hour, they say, I came out into the world. The midwife then arrived in time to cut the cord.

I did not end up marrying my great-aunt's son, but I did pick up on the vibes of optimism, wealth, and happiness that I was born into. That, along with my lineage — my great grandmother Maria was a wealthy, well-respected healer — gave me the sense of nobility that our more difficult days to come could not, it seems, take away from me.

Going deeper and deeper within, I knew I was blocking my relationship with my power animal. I decided to be still inside

and wear him the way I do my skin. From the feet, or paws, up-
ward, his skin and fur began to reach up my body, going higher
and higher until I wore his face and saw through his eyes. I saw
what I was afraid of. The wild side of me, the fierce part that
wanted to run and run. Not run away. Just run with joy through
the pastures.

"You're getting your child energy back," Fiona said when I
shared my experience.

"Yes, my child energy before it got poked left and right with
do's and don'ts. What scared me about becoming the wolf had
nothing to do with calling it near me and petting it. My wild
side was once not well directed. I've tamed myself a great deal,
and while I don't want to be completely untamed, I want to find
the balance so that I can create extraordinary work during my
untamed time, to really lose myself, but to also catch my prey."

"Wonderful! Wonderful realization! Great work!"

"I had tried to control my writing spirit, the way I had done
with my home, to please the critics. And it never really worked
anyway."

The next time I sat at my desk, I entered the dreamscape
through my wolf. In the dreamscape, I became vulnerable and
free. My words ran through the pages of the story that stalked
me night and day. I seized the story, ate the story, and we became one.

Chapter 15
OLD FRIENDSHIPS

"Do you mind if I eat my dinner while you talk?" Fiona asked when I called her.

"Not at all," I said.

Fiona had been gone for a while, first on vacation and then for her daughter's wedding in Vancouver, which was so intimate it consisted of only 20 guests – I think that might have included the bride and groom. She told me to check out the pictures on her Facebook page once we were done talking.

I then told her about a dinner I had Friday night at Mon Jin Lau, an Asian restaurant whose name translates to "House of Ten Thousand Jewels." It has been around for over four decades, but this was my first time in it. I walked into the Zen-like atmosphere with eclectic rhythms. It was pretty dim, but I was able to spot my three friends sitting in a corner table. They all got up when they saw me, and we screamed in excitement as we hugged and kissed each other, giving one another compliments on how good we looked and how little we had changed. We had not sat together like this in fifteen years, and we were meeting because one of them was getting married and moving to another state.

We were excited to share stories about our children and husbands, or in one woman's case, an ex-husband. We brought up hilarious incidences from our pasts, made fun of each other, and complained about the difficulty of motherhood. With the exception of the bride-to-be, we all had children and were doing juggling acts raising them. We then talked about marriage and how that was work in itself.

"You guys are scaring me," said the bride-to-be. "Should I be walking down the aisle?"

We all laughed.

"For me, marriage is less work than being single because there's so much more meaning in it," I said. "And since you survived singlehood for almost forty years, you'll be fine as a wife."

We discussed this topic a little further before she invited us to her bachelorette party, assuring us there would be no strippers. It's pretty rare for an Arabic bachelorette party to have a stripper. For my bachelorette party, when my nieces had me sit down on a chair and blindfolded my eyes, I got nervous that they'd broken their promise and brought a stripper. The only thing that eased my worry was the presence of my mom, my uncle's ex-wife, and his widow. The young ones would not dare bring a male stripper around the elderly pack of women. Hearing the chaos and excitement, I wondered what was up their sleeves. Then one of my cousins appeared in a red and black corset lingerie and did the most graceful strip tease I'd ever seen.

Our dinners then arrived. I had the Hunan crispy chicken and shared an order of sushi with the bride-to-be. We took bites from each other's plates, and we all agreed my Hunan chicken was the tastiest. Continuing with our stories, we laughed until our stomachs hurt. It was the first time in a long while where I had spent time away from family and work and was so relaxed that I did not want to leave. I savored the moment, reliving the attitude of my early twenties, when such outings were the norm.

I woke up before seven o'clock the next morning and sat

outside under the orange August sun. The beauty of the night before rotated around my heart. I felt like a rotisserie chicken, basted with love and compassion and slowly cooked to perfection. Such evenings must be repeated! Maybe this was the group I was looking for. I needed adult interaction with mature women who shared years of sisterhood with me. These women were it! We had gone to college together, cried on each other's shoulders, and were a support system when breakups occurred.

I reclined in my chair in utter joy and satisfaction to have finally found my circle. A black and a gray squirrel chased each other over my lawn. I took my eyes off my notebook and followed the squirrels' playfulness. I was on the lookout for the reddish-brown colored squirrel that normally accompanied them when the phone rang. Seeing it was one of the three wonderful friends, I answered with the best of moods.

"I don't like your post," she said shortly after our hellos, in a directness that belonged to that of a teacher from a dictatorial country.

"What?" I asked, caught off guard.

"The post you wrote on your blog about the bride being scared and all that. I don't like it. It was inappropriate, and you should remove it."

What on earth was she talking about?

I had started a blog on the first day of January and called it *Cultural Glimpse*. In it I wrote about the exquisite places, people, and things I met, visited, and experienced in my neighborhood. Unless it addressed a political issue, my posts were filled with positive energy and oftentimes humor. Normally I received a "Thank you" or dinner invitations or little gifts like chocolate for what I wrote. The blog was inspired by words my Native American teacher Chip often said to me. "If you stand on the corner of New York long enough, you'll see the whole world."

In this particular case, I had mentioned that the married women had complained so much about kids, cleaning, and housewife duties that we frightened the bride-to-be to where she may change her mind about this marriage business. But then I added, "Luckily, the groom is such a great catch, there's no way she would back out." I had actually paid her fiancé a compliment.

Feeling uncomfortable, I changed the subject. "I tried to befriend you on Facebook but couldn't find your name."

"Yeah, well, I was going to send you an invite, but when I saw that post..." she began. "Even the bride's family and friends saw it, and let's just say they were not too pleased."

"You're joking?"

"I'm not."

"So are you calling me on her behalf or on your behalf?"

"I did have a chance to discuss this with her, and she feels the same way. But she did not ask me to call. I decided to do that on my own."

I quickly got off the phone with her, called the bride-to-be, and asked, "Is all this true?"

She explained that, yes, it most definitely was. Family, friends, and future in-laws were contacting her to find out if she was calling off the wedding. The fiancé was offended that she was getting cold feet.

"But there was no mention of you getting cold feet or the wedding being called off," I said. "I was making fun of the married women's hectic life and actually complimenting your fiancé by saying he was a great catch."

"My fiancé and people saw it differently," she said.

Something seemed odd about this whole thing. It was Saturday morning, the sun barely having risen, and the blog post was not posted until after 2:30 am, when 80 percent of the state's population was sound asleep. How did the people in her world have the chance to read it, turn into frenzy, and contact this bride-to-be as fast if a war had broken out?

"Oh, you'd be surprised how quick news spreads through social media," she said to that.

At this point, I apologized profusely and promised to change the post. The moment I did that, I reddened with fury and regretted having apologized. I had done nothing wrong except for follow my passion, writing. The first woman who called me had received a journalism degree, which she never used. The bride-to-be had dropped out of law school. They'd given up on their dreams, and that was not my fault.

Nothing had changed. No wonder I had distanced myself from these women for so long. Most of them did not show up to celebrate my milestones, but they did not pass up the opportunity to spoil our wonderful evenings by pointing out that I had done something wrong. They were always waiting for me to trip, and even if I did not trip, they still poked at who I am and picked on me. In my culture, women put on a façade. They live a double life. Living an honest, sincere life, being comfortable with who you are, is not the norm.

"Yeah, so I guess the wedding nearly went kaput because of my post," I said to Fiona.

"As you raise your vibrations and get to know who you are, the people who you were friends with may fall off because your energy and their energy is at a different place," she said. "They are trying to lower your vibration down. Now you can lower your vibration to what they're comfortable with or you can raise your vibrations higher and bring theirs up. Neither is right or wrong."

"What bothers me is that I responded by changing the post and even apologizing!"

"It's a hook, and they're trying to pull you down. Undo the hook and pull yourself up. How are you going to pull yourself up?"

"I don't know. The bride's bachelorette party is coming up. I already RSVP'd, saying I was coming. Deep down I don't want to go and deal with them. But I'm afraid that if I don't go I'll look like a coward, as if I'm ashamed of something."

"So what will you do?"

"Go to the bachelorette party."

"How is that going to pull you up?"

"It's not! What I really want to do is not go. I don't want to be in this small intimate group which I feel I don't belong in, but I'm only going out of obligation even though I'm no longer at a point where I do things out of just that."

"That's raising your vibration. You're telling the universe I'm not going back to sleep and I'm going to show you how I'm not going back to sleep. Your friends won't be able to identify exactly what's happening. They won't know why they're reacting the way they are reacting. They are unconscious. They are not awake. They can't help what they're doing. They can't really pull you down but you chose to be pulled down. It happens instantly. You realized it later, and now you're conscious."

"I realized it the moment I hung up the phone, and I was angry and fuming about it."

"You don't need to beat yourself up because you fell asleep for a second. Are you going to go back to sleep?"

"No!"

"You were aware what was happening but fear was preventing you from speaking it. You needed to pull up your strength. Don't deny yourself the truth that you knew unless you want to. But I think you're dishonoring yourself by doing that."

"Deep down I see myself as not going," I said. "I know that's the right answer, but I'm afraid to put my foot down."

"You don't have to put your foot down. Just bow out. Do it with grace. Curtsy out."

"I like that," I said. "But what excuse should I give?"

"You're split because your mind is still in the past where you have to make an excuse that they will invalidate anyway. You don't have to make an excuse or lie; that's lowering your vibration. Just say I don't want to come or I can't come."

If only I did not have to be so pretentious in order to please others, I would soar like a bird into my dreams. "I've had to explain myself and my actions to so many people over the years that it has become a habit," I said. "Rarely were they sympathetic toward whatever I said anyway. All I should have done is speak the truth – I don't want to or I can't."

"These are lower vibration hooks."

"I was thinking, do you think this matter is petty?"

"I don't think you need to think about it," she said.

I laughed.

"What you might want to ask yourself is what is it inside of me that makes me perceive this is petty? When I look at it, I don't see that it was petty. Look at the lesson in that and look at how you could turn this around."

I thought about it and came up with nothing. "I don't know."

She remained silent, forcing me to continue to look into myself.

"You know, when I first told my sister about this, she was

initially upset and said I shouldn't go to the bachelorette party, but later she softened up and figured, well, I could go and she would come with me because she's invited too, and we could just ignore the girls with the righteous attitude who called me out about the blog post." I pressed my knees to my chest and curled my arms around them. "That's not me anymore, where I have to pretend with people I don't care to pursue a relationship with. Why should I let this go when they couldn't let the thing about the post go? They are the ones who instigated this situation, and all I'm doing is honoring myself."

"Ho!" she said, which indicates an Amen in our circle.

I asked that we please move on and talk about the next assignment, which was about gathering the right stones and crystals. How would I know which was right for me?

Fiona said, "If a stone catches your eye, hold it up and ask it, 'Do you want to teach me something? Do you want me to take you home with me?'" She told me a story of when she was a little girl, skipping stones by the lake. "The ones that really wanted to return to the water would call me out. They were calling me to be the vehicle, to move them because they can't move themselves."

She suggested that when I go into a shop looking for the right crystals to close my eyes, put my hand in the container of crystals or stones, and see if I can feel it vibrating. "Is it making your hands warm or is your body heat making it warm?" she said. "Ask it, 'Stone, do you want me to take you home?'"

She and I went through the book, *The Crystal Bible*. She suggested I look in the appendix section for the words throat chakra. Under that heading, I best related to the word "unblocking" because I still felt that my literary voice was blocked. On page forty-one was a picture and description of a blue lace agate, said to be a powerful throat healer.

"What you might want to do is take that blue lace crystal, put it in a pouch, or make a necklace out of it," she said. "Eventually, have a stone that would work on each chakra. Lay them on your body as you go to sleep. Sleep with them on your body. While you meditate, the stone will fall off when it has taken enough energy for that session. To pick it up is not allowing it to do its job. In my case the third eye crystal fell off immediately. It is also good to have crystals in your house.

"You can use stone for grounding," she said. "Ninety percent of the time I have it in my pocket. When I'm feeling I'm getting scattered, they're driving me crazy at work, or I'm driving myself crazy, I put my hand in my pocket and rub it. That's the energy I asked them to have for me because you can program them."

"I can't wait to shop for the right crystals and stones."

"And your kids will have a blast."

Yes, my kids! Where in heaven's name were they and what were they doing? I heard a serious cry from my son and headed toward the area it was coming from, the garage. On the way, my daughter told me to hurry. There was a chair by the bathroom closet with a pink Dora stepping stool on top of it. She had obviously tried to grab a band aid for her brother. In the garage, there was a folding chair next to the food shelf.

"What happened?" I asked my son as he jumped up and down in pain, tears rushing down his face.

They explained that the chair had pinched his finger when he tried to close the door.

"What's the Band-Aid for?" I asked my daughter, who had placed three Band-Aids on her chin.

"I got a little scratch."

I kissed my son's finger, gave him an ice pack, and returned to my room with him beside me. I held him in my arms and asked Fiona, "Do you know what?"

"No, I don't."

"I just realized from the look of that blue lace agate that what I need to learn is to speak my truth but to speak it gently. Because I bite my tongue often, react nicely, and pretend something does not bother me when it absolutely does, my feelings get bottled up, and when I finally speak up I come off strong and angry. So rather than resolve issues, I create them by holding back because I am unable to express my hurts truthfully."

"Ho!" she said, then asked, "Do you know what?"

"No, I don't."

"This dis ease has become a beautiful gift, hasn't it?"

"You just turned this around for me!"

"No, you did," she said. "If you put this on the death side of the altar – on the death side put whatever it is that is driving you crazy and balance it out on the life side with all those things shown to you – then all of a sudden, it's like you're seeing the beauty and the light in the shadow."

After we hung up, I opened Fiona's Facebook page and pictures of an extraordinarily elegant outdoor wedding appeared. I saw Fiona for the first time. Although we were Facebook friends, her profile picture had been too blurry, or my mind was, for me to make out her features. Her strong femininity took me by surprise. She had salt and pepper short hair, grey and silver with black streaks. Her face glowed with confidence and happiness, like a pot of gold shining under a bright sun. Her toned couture body had on a long floral dress. The blue shawl over her shoulders added to the femininity.

In one picture, she stood proudly next to her two sons and

her daughter, the bride. Another picture was of her, her mother, and her daughter. My mentors led such a normal life, or so it seemed from the outside. In spirit, they belonged to another world. They spoke a language that was fried in dreams, mysteries, and magic, a language that bloomed with creativity, that inspired love. Yet they lived a normal life. They had admirable jobs and pleasant families.

Chapter 16
WOLVES

By July, we, Lynn's apprentices, were to have developed a daily practice that would become a routine for us. We were to follow certain activities that made our day feel sacred and balanced, such as sitting in silence and pulling a card from The Power Deck each day, an ancient oracular system of affirmations and meditations. A silent harmony sustained me while the hot temperatures of summer aroused a gust of activity in the people around me. My spirit moved into the school work with confidence and force and avoided negativity.

"I've been having a most magical time," said the woman from Colorado.

We were on the phone after doing a second meditation with our power animals.

"A woman who knew that I had my Australian shaman, Morning Star, stay at my house for a month brought me an owl she'd found on the road, a great horned owl," she said. "I'm going to make a feather fan from its feathers."

"How did the owl die?" I asked.

"It had a broken wing and must have been hit by a car. I'm taking it in and honoring it. It's illegal to have this owl, to have a rapture feather, unless you're a Native American. The woman who gifted it to me took it to a taxidermist - you know, a person who mounts the skin of animals. He said he can't have it. He told her, 'You need to put it on the side of the road.' She didn't want to leave it on the road or bury it, so she brought it to me. It was hard to cut the wings."

Her voice had a calm quality. She behaved as if she had found a diamond and was pleased but not too surprised.

"A lot of animals are presenting themselves to me: ox, snakes, and now the owl," she said. "I saw six hawks today. Hawks are spirit messengers. I've had a black fox cross my path. The tip of its tail was white and fluffy. No one else in the area saw it. I looked it up, and the source said there were only four or five spotted in Colorado. There used to be lots of black foxes in Europe, but they were killed for their fur."

Her story mesmerized me. When my sisters or friends talked on the phone, the last thing we mentioned were which animals crossed our path. We talked about the day's events, our children, and other women.

"I heard you and your husband went swimming with the dolphins," I said. "Where was that? I'd love to do that someday."

"We had to go to a little island on Fort Lauderdale in the English Waters. It's illegal to swim with them in the United States."

So many rules and regulations regarding animals!

"Dolphins are like people," she said. "They are connected to spirit."

The last thing she told me before we hung up was how she did her water ceremony by the water. She lay by the water and let the water go over her, and when she opened her eyes she saw a snake. The snake went beneath her clothes, which she had placed on the side. Snakes are about shedding and transformation.

After we hung up, I thought about the apprentice's home in Colorado and her experiences with the animals. It reminded me of Lynn's books, where she described her Native American teachers' homes in northern Canada. Agnes Whistling Elk and Ruby Plenty Chiefs lived in the boondocks, or so it seemed, with regions that had unfamiliar physical and spiritual landscapes. There was a substance in their world that could clear many ailments, including depression.

I poured water in a cup and stuck it in the microwave, then went over my notes. The message my power animal, the wolf, had given me, through her, was, "I am beautiful, like you. We are a reflection of each other. I love my family and protect them like you do yours. I am here for your strength whenever you need me. Just call me, invite me in."

The microwave timer beeped. I added a teaspoon of Nescafé into the boiling water and noticed two slices of breads left in the toaster from the night before. They were as hard as cardboard. I took them outside for the squirrel awaiting me in the tree house and threw the toast in his direction. He quickly picked one of them up, went to the edge of the fence, and nibbled noisily. I was videotaping him with my iPhone when suddenly he dropped the toast. It went into the neighbor's backyard. He looked at me like "Ooops!" and rushed after it. I laughed heartily.

I sat in the patio and stared ahead, reflecting on all the talk about wolves. Earlier this week an apprentice from Germany whom I did this same mediation with had a similar message for me from my power animal. She said that my wolf seemed lonely. His fur was scrubby.

She wrote me an email that said, "He enjoys being caressed, his fur being stroked. He likes being taken care of by you. You and he will not be lonely anymore. At some point, I saw you running with him across the plains, being free! You were his power. He was later on top of a mountain, howling very, very powerfully, and I asked him what kind of power he stood for. He said it was about communication, being heard far away. You have a message to tell and write. The message is important for a large space, for the universe. It is going to be a 'wolf message.' Focused. Raw. Strong."

I thought deeply about the apprentices' messages. *What did all this mean? How could I strengthen my relationship with the wolf when I was afraid of animals?* The Arab world was not into keeping pets. I was afraid of dogs, whose origin began with the domestication of the Grey Wolf tens of thousands of years ago. Twice I was chased by them. Once in Baghdad, a small but loud barking dog chased me all the way into my house, where I entered a bathroom and locked the door until my cousin came to rescue me. A second time was in my first year in Michigan, during my walk to school. I was bundled up in a winter coat, gloves, and a hat, walking on snow when suddenly a big dog, a Komondor, came after me. Screaming, I ran as quickly as I could until I reached the crossing guard. She hugged me, and I remember her having a slight smile, maybe thinking I had over-reacted because of my unfamiliarity with pets. I cried into her embrace until the dog was out of sight.

My manuscript came to mind. The editor returned it the night before with nine pages of critique. Her heavy comments indicated I clearly had a lot of work ahead of me. I sat under the sun in the backyard, looking at the even clouds in the sky. My mind dropped to the center of my being, into a deep silence, and it became still. I focused on my breathing, focusing and breathing, focusing and breathing, until I walked to a decision. I decided to symbolically wear my wolf mask once again, to shred the manuscript to pieces and then make it whole again.

That night my husband and I rented movies. The kids

watched their movie and ate popcorn in the living room while my husband made himself a drink and prepared my water pipe. He and I then sat outside on the patio. We were happy. He had received a new date for his immigration test. The letter brought more relief than I imagined it would. It was as if someone had removed a cork off the arteries of our hearts. We still did not feel comfortable enough to talk about the process, so I updated him on what my agent said about my work. She had shown my feature script to a producer in Hollywood and he loved it, said that this had a lot of commercial potential.

"*Inshallah*, God will open doors for you," he said.

"It's frustrating, always getting very close, then nothing."

He dipped a kettle chip into the yogurt. "You know that your work is like that," he said. "It's not as though you have a nine-to-five job or a business where certain money comes in and goes out. You need one door to open and you're all set."

"It feels as though that door is barely moving."

"Say '*Ya Allah*' and it'll all work out. Just have faith and patience."

I smoked the water pipe and observed the clouds which earlier were tinted with a reddish color by the sun behind them. A few airplanes passed by. The tree leaves ruffled, a cat cried, or maybe laughed, as time passed in silence.

"Why do we have to wait so long to spend time alone like this?" I asked.

He looked at me, threw a few cussing words in Arabic, and swore to God that I'm crazy.

Smiling, I deeply inhaled the scent that emanated from the golden-apple flavored coal on the foil. "I keep telling you how important it is for me to have one-on-one time with you. Yet whenever there's an opportunity for us to go out you invite the whole world to come along."

He swore again. "You're crazy, you know that?"

"Why? Because I want to spend alone time with my husband?"

"Don't you see that I work all day and barely have time to eat dinner, watch a little television, and go to sleep?"

"I'm not asking for every day, not even once a week. Once a month would be great, but even that doesn't happen. It's always family gatherings, family outings, going out with couples, etc., etc. You make time for everyone except for me."

"What are you talking about? The few times I've gone out to dinner with my friends? On those days, you are like a queen, exhilarated because then you don't have to cook dinner for me."

He grabbed seeds from a bowl, cracked them, and threw the shell in the round glass ashtray. His knitted brows and the swiftness in which he cracked the shells emphasized the wisdom he had just shared. "You never say thank you, God, for giving me a husband who works hard and provides for his family, whose feet hurt because he's standing up all day working."

"I do thank God, but not in that Arabic way that you're describing now. Look, I know that even though we have the same backgrounds, we grew up in different cultures. In Iraq, dating is not the norm. The rules are, you don't date when you're single and normally you do not arrange dates with your wife or husband." I blew smoke into his face. "I'm not asking for every day. All I'm asking for is this, what we're experiencing right now."

He stared at me, grinning. "You're crazy, you know that?"

I blew more smoke into his dark and handsome face. "Yes, I know."

Later in bed, I asked him if he'd ever seen a wolf.

"Yes, a lot of them," he said. "I've killed them, too."

"Why?" I asked, surprised.

"They used to eat the neighbor's cattle. Sometimes they would eat children."

"Were they vicious?"

"Yes. They only came out at night. The only thing we saw were their brown eyes glistening in the dark. When we shot, we didn't know if we hit the target or not."

"What else did you shoot?" I asked.

"Everything. My favorite was trapping ducks. We had wild dogs that we had to shoot too. They once came into our yard and ate our deer. We heard the barking and her crying. My father went out there and shot two of the dogs."

"I didn't think people in Iraq kept pets."

"Oh yeah they did. We had a deer, birds. A lot of stray cats would wander near our home. We'd shoot them because they tried to eat our birds."

I was quiet.

"Why do you ask about the wolf?"

"Just wondering," I said.

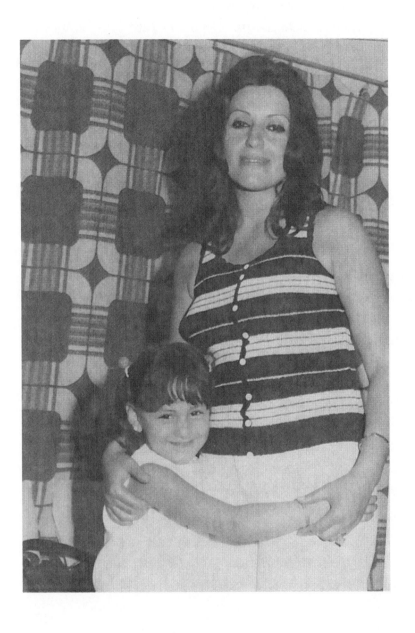

Chapter 17
KEEPER OF THE TREE

For years we have made it a tradition to spend a summer weekend at Kalahari waterpark in Ohio with my extended family. The resort is named after the Kalahari Desert in southern Africa and has African-themed designs and events. The artwork in their lobbies and guestrooms were imported from local markets and shops in Africa. Our families looked forward to this time despite the chaos we experienced when trying to arrange the trip, and the barrel of responsibility fell upon me due to my computer literacy and my history of traveling.

The morning of our departure my daughter and I stepped out onto the patio. I rubbed jasmine oil on her long hair as we took in the sound of birds chirping, the smell of jasmine, and the warm morning sun against our backs. I caught a glimpse of myself in the glass door, and I saw my daughter as an adult. One day she would reflect on this day, similarly to the many times I reflected on the days I had lived under my mother's roof: the safety, the peace, the delicious food.

A large bumble bee came at us. "I think it's attracted to the smell of jasmine oil," I said, hurrying my daughter back into the house.

The cars carrying the people going to Kalahari arrived at my home. Children jumped out, excited to see their cousins. Adults came into the house to use the bathroom. Someone asked for a thread and needle. Someone else wanted a safety pin. I went through each room to make sure we did not forget anything and that the electricity and stove were turned off. I was the last to walk out.

"I feel bad for Mom," Niran said when she saw me. "When I dropped her off at our sister's house, she started to cry. I told her, 'Mom, it's not too late. You can still come with us if you want to. Your stuff is all packed.' She said, 'No, no. I can't come.'"

"You should have insisted that she come," I said.

"It's not that she couldn't come. It's that she felt bad that she can't come with us anymore."

I held back tears as I went into our minivan. A train of five cars followed each other, and we headed south toward Detroit. Despite the boisterous attitude of everyone in our car and the neighboring cars carrying relatives, I felt incredible sadness about my mother's deteriorating health. It worsened each day, preventing her from joining in some of our trips and events. When she left my brother's home, her voice became awfully quiet, even absent. Her strength began to dissolve, like water, into the pores of the earth.

She used to come to Kalahari with us every year. She did not swim or sunbathe or do anything but sit under the large umbrella and watch us from afar, embroidered with a smile of pride. We would reserve a table in the corner, near the exit door, and she would sit and keep an eye on our items as we went back and forth. Occasionally she walked to the edge of the pools, where the water ran free, and allowed for her feet to get wet. Nowadays she was so fragile that we would not be able to leave her for long periods of time. She might not even be able to handle the two-and-a-half-hour drive. A week ago my sister had called and said, "Mom fell off the edge of the bed, and I can't get her up. Can you please come help me?"

By the time I got there, she had been sitting on the floor for over an hour. After I helped get her up, I went into the bathroom and cried. I wiped my eyes as best as I could and washed my face so my mother would not see that I had cried. When I returned to the living room, she motioned for me to sit beside her on the couch. Once I sat beside her, she placed her hand over mine as if to say "I love you" and "thank you." With her sitting on my left side and my daughter sitting on my right side, I felt light and happy, as if the wilds of winter were suddenly gulped by a guardian angel. That night, I dreamt that my mother was living at her first cousin's house, the daughter of the woman who helped my mother give birth to me. I was glad that she was happy, safe, and well taken care of.

Shortly into our drive, I set my intent for the trip. I brought along Lynn's *Writing Spirit*, the book that started it all. I planned to reread it, then bask in the sun and allow my writing spirit to be nice and ripe by the time I returned home so that I could begin to revise the manuscript, and revise well. I would reconcile with the pains of long ago and bathe myself in the heat of what brought me to this career in the first place: the calling, love, and sacredness.

At the resort, I walked around with the book in my hand and memories of my mother's energy when she used to come along with us. How I love and miss her, I thought as I held back tears. Something about her absence and her coming closer to death caused me to more fully seize life's fleeting moments, connecting me more closely to life and its mystery.

I surrendered to the scorching sun and the hot sand grains beneath my feet, feeling the fires of love slowly burn the hidden fears within me. I surrendered to the clear blue pool water, swimming through new dreams that nourished and fulfilled me. I surrendered to the pages of Lynn's book, devouring the exquisite words of several passages. One in particular which helped me enter a vast sea of the subconscious was on page 221, where she wrote, "As a writer, you become an alchemist as you take the world of the ordinary and transform it into mystery, when you take ordinary words and transform them into expressions of great beauty and wisdom and joy, when you are able to so entertain your readers that they perhaps lose all sense of time because they do not want to put your writing down."

Three days of drinking the essence of such messages, of allowing the sun, water, sand, air, and other natural ingredients to enhance my mood, and I returned home under the spell of a goddess that ruled herself by a balanced feminine and masculine powers.

* * *

"I'm dying," Cicily cried into the phone, her voice barely audible.

I sat on my bed and wiped tears from my face. "Don't say that. You'll be fine. You have to stay strong for your daughters. Promise me you'll stay strong."

"I've done everything I can. I have no strength left in me."

Since we met, Cicily had been in and out of hospitals. Her medical problems started long ago, and her diagnosis was a mystery. She had one surgery after another. A mutual friend kept everyone informed through group emails. Each update made me more concerned, and I wondered what would happen to Cicily's daughters if, God forbid, she died. Facebook posts kept popping up, one announcement of bad news after another. I wanted to help but did not know how. When I discussed her condition with Leslie, my first-year mentor, to learn how I could possibly help, she had said, "You need to first find out why this woman wants to die."

I had no clue, so I asked Cicily. She had no clue. She figured it was her fate and in no way generated by her. Nine months of watching this situation go from bad to worse and the words the Lebanese-American filmmaker said to me last year resonated once again. "Rather than being a businesswoman, you are behaving as a nurturing mother to everyone involved, caring for this and that person's delinquencies rather than moving the project forward."

Bonnie came to mind, the woman who, for years, gave herself the title of a producer on my film project, claimed she was revirginized thanks to surgery, and caused all sorts of shenanigans that nearly ruined my name in the professional community. *Have I once again attracted a wounded woman instead of a business partner?* I ignored this question since my manuscript was still incomplete and busied myself with writing and schoolwork. A lot of assignments had to be tended to, including one called "Keeper of the Language of the Trees." I asked Fiona how I should do this assignment.

"Go to the park, sit against a tree, and begin observing what is around you," she said. "Feel energy going up and down the tree and feel your feet against the soil. Maybe as you leave, pull a hair out and leave it there as a giveaway. It can even be corn meal, or anything."

"Why is it called *Keeper of the Trees*?"

"Ask the tree why it's called *Keeper of the Trees*. All the questions you're asking me are perfect questions to ask the tree. You can ramble off whatever you want and ask the tree if it's willing to help. It may say hey, go to the tree twenty feet down the road, it can better help you."

I laughed at that idea. In cartoons for children, talking to animals and trees was quite natural and innocent, but for adults such a reality was often considered fiction or maddening. During our moment of silence, I lit another incense stick as the last one had vanished and watched the line of smoke shoot straight up like a school ruler. I returned to the bed, and soon my son joined me, kicking his foot into my thighs and bumping his head against my iPhone. Then Fiona asked, "So what did you decide about the bachelorette party. Are you going?"

"Well…"

"Remember," she said. "There's no right or wrong answer."

"The other day I was at the mall, and I saw the cutest dress…"

We laughed wholeheartedly.

After we hung up, I gathered my kids and put them in the bathtub, thinking, I must reclaim the things needed for my act of power to finish the book. I must keep looking for something or someone to rescue me, to help me get to where I want to go. But all I have right now is me and God, the essential power in this universe that infuses us with life even when we feel dead.

"Mamma, can I pray in the bathtub?" my son asked. "And in the end say, amen?" He blinked cutely.

"Yes," I said, smiling.

"Mamma, do grownups grow up?"

"Yes, in a different way."

Later, I asked him what he meant by that.

"When grownups grow up, do they go back to normal?"

I laughed.

"Why are you laughing?" he asked.

I kept laughing.

"I love you forever," he said.

"I love you forever, too."

I did *Keeper of the Language of the Trees* outside the Warren Civic Center, in their little park area. I sat against the husk of a huge tree near the stream, which had two giant roots visibly stretching into the earth. My children picked up sticks and stones and they ran around in circles. I took in a few deep breaths, not knowing what to expect. I had never given trees this much attention, unless they carried a desired fruit or had a story associated to them. Trees have played an important role in many of the world's mythologies and religions and have been given deep, sacred meanings throughout the ages. Many people see them as a powerful symbol of growth, decay, and resurrection. Christianity and Islam treated the worship of trees as idolatry, and this led to their destruction in Europe and most of West Asia.

Yet trees have served people by providing food, oxygen, wood, paper – giving, giving, giving, and not asking anything in return. Trees grow faster the older they get, but they expand wider, not taller, with age. They resemble mothers in many ways. They give and give of themselves, they expand spirituality and often physically, and both do not really receive the honor they deserve. How little we reward what sustains us and instead are ready to exploit it by cutting it from its roots or by accusing mothers to be the cause of human destruction because her gender ate an apple.

The wind blew west, and my deceased sister's spirit came forth, taking me by surprise. I had not thought about Basima for a while. The breeze whirled around my cheeks, shining light on a day when I was visiting Iraq in the spring of 2000. One night, two male cousins who were close to my age, in their mid to late twenties, took me for a walk on a main road in Baghdad. We passed the merchants sitting on chairs near their carts, selling food, colas, flowers, wallets, or small items like pens. One of my cousins, Firas, stopped at an ice cream parlor and ordered three cups of ice cream.

"Do you know where Basima's house is?" I asked Bashar, the other cousin. I had heard that, although my sister had passed away in the early 1990s and her children have since then left the country, the house was inhabited by her in-laws.

"Oh sure!" he said, excited. "It's only a ten minute walking distance from here."

"Really?" I was certain he was exaggerating.

"I swear to you. We used to visit them, and they visited us all the time."

Firas returned and handed each one of us a cup of ice cream. I asked Bashar, "Can you take me there now?"

"Where?" Firas asked.

"Basima's house," I said.

"Well..." As Bashar wrestled with the idea, Firas said, "Yes, we can go."

"My mom would kill me if she knew I took you there," Bashar said.

"Why?" I asked.

"It's getting pretty late. I was supposed to have you home an hour ago."

"There's nothing to worry about," Firas said. "She's with both of us. Let's go."

We crossed a busy intersection and walked into a quiet

subdivision, the whole time Bashar making me swear and re-swear that I would not tell his mother, who was also my maternal aunt, he had brought me here. While in Baghdad, I stayed at his mother's home. He also lived there with his wife and toddler son. I repeatedly promised him to rest assured that I would not say a word.

It did not take long to reach my sister's front gate. Bashar rang the doorbell. We heard footsteps coming toward the gate. A woman asked who we were, and Bashar said, "This is Bashar. Weam, Basima's sister, is here from America."

She opened the gate and looked at me in astonishment. It was Sameera. I remembered her from old photographs. She was twenty years older now, but she did not look much different than before. She had remained single her whole life and therefore devoted herself to caring for her brothers' children. Sameera opened the gate wide for us to enter. The moment I stepped into the front yard, I recalled my visits here as a child. I used to go on the swing with my niece, who was six months my senior. I had even spent a few nights here, one of which got me in trouble with the elementary school principal because I did not attend Saddam's parade. In front of all the students who stood in line after having recited the national anthem, she had slapped me so hard that I passed out. This story migrated with me to the United States and, like maple syrup in a jar, preserved itself in my heart for decades thereafter.

We went into the living room. Sameera wanted to hurry into the kitchen to make coffee, but I begged her not to because our visit would be short and I didn't want a moment wasted. She succumbed and sat in front of me, still shocked by my presence, as if I was a ghost. We asked each other about our welfare and the welfare of our families, and midway through moving my lips and watching her move hers, the energy of my sister and my childhood tiptoed into the air, smelling like perfume. It dawned on me that this was the room I played in with my niece when I was a child.

I looked around the room. A large-framed black and white photo of my sister hanging on the wall caught my attention. A chill passed through me before it was put out by her smooth and gentle memory. My tears then broke free, and I dropped my face into the palm of my hands. Sameera followed my behavior, and in unison, we lamented my sister's loss.

The men sat in silence and sadness, their head bowed. Soon Bashar reminded me it was time to leave. I obliged, although I wished to stay here longer and continue to feel the spirit of my sister. Before we left, Sameera said that I must return to spend a few nights. I said I would.

Outside the active streets had evaporated into idleness. The high spirits I had earlier shrunk in size, going from a large rock to a tiny pebble. I could barely hear Bashar's continuous statements that I tell no one where we had been. He behaved as though he had taken me to Cairo to visit the pharaohs' tombs, not a few streets down to visit the house my sister once lived in. I simply nodded at his pleas, my feet slowing down, my mind trying to leave the past and catch up with the moment.

We arrived to my aunt's house. As we entered the front door, we were greeted by my aunt, who stood on the left side, and Bashar's wife, who stood on the right side. They looked as stern as the guards at Buckingham Palace with their gaze piercing through Bashar like that of an eagle. I continued inside, but the women detained Bashar for interrogation. Within fifteen seconds – yes, seconds, not minutes – Bashar fessed up. Step-by-step he described to his mother and wife where we had gone and what we had done. The women then reprimanded him for having subjected me to sadness.

Before my trip to Iraq was over, I spent a few nights at the house Basima once lived in, where a picture of her still lives. I also had a cousin take me to Basima's grave. The cemetery contained graves built with baked bricks and plaster, and it rose at different levels. Among the tombstones were room-size family crypts built by the wealthy, often topped by domes. My sister's husband had bought the family crypt so their whole family would be buried there. He did not know then that his family would scatter to different parts of the world due to Iraq's political uncertainties, mainly wars.

Engraved on my sister's tombstone was one request, that her children would be well-taken care of.

Chapter 18
THE STORY CONTINUES TO CONTINUE

After the "due to unforeseen circumstances" letter, my husband and I held our breath and spent the next few months going to church every Sunday. Then another letter arrived with a new scheduled interview. We held our breaths even tighter, and the day before his interview, we got into a huge argument. He had taken the day off from work so he could study and I could help him review for the test. After we'd gone over the first 100 questions, we started on the writing test. He explained which section I had to recite, but unaware of this written test as I did not have to take it during my naturalization exam, I made my own suggestions. He became upset that I was not listening, I made a few jokes, and he got very angry. I threw the test down on the coffee table, went to the kitchen and said I would no longer help him. I began washing the breakfast dishes, loudly slamming each one into the dish rack.

"I've been waiting thirteen years for this day and you turn it into a joke!" he finally said.

I dropped the dish in my hand into the sink and leaned against the counter to face him. "You talk as if you're the only one who has suffered through this process. Since that day at immigration, I have blocked any ideas about traveling outside this country. I have spent half the time worrying that someone would find and use any excuse to deport you and I would lose a husband and my children would lose a father. Remember the day you went to Montreal? They stopped you at the airport and wanted to detain you because you had on you a travel document but not a green card. I just about died. I felt so sick, my whole body was shaking. I thought for sure I would not see you again. Thank God they were decent enough to get you on the next flight back to Michigan!"

He lowered his head.

"Your status affected my status," I said. "I had to work hard to remind myself I was an American, and I became too afraid to write."

He looked up at me, his eyes red. "You were afraid to write?"

"Yes, I was! I still wrote, but the joy was gone. I had lost my voice, because I felt as if there were eyes inside my computer disapprovingly watching my thoughts through my words. I was afraid I would piss someone off with the wrong comment, and my punishment would be to deny you your citizenship."

I was much calmer now, feeling bad for the both of us. After wiping my hands with a towel, I returned to the couch beside him and picked up the test. "So are you going to apologize so we can go back to the test?" I asked.

He smiled. "I'm sorry, and I love you."

"I know you're scared, but so am I. You know when Dawn tells me her prison stories, on many levels I can relate because my heart, mind, and spirit have been in prison for almost seven years." I thought about the Hanna family's resignation to Dawn's prison term. She had recently lost the appeal. "Dawn still has another year or so to go, but we're almost done."

"God willing," he said.

I took the kids to church and spent two-and-a-half hours

writing at McDonald's. At home, we ate the barbecue that my husband had made and went to bed early.

"Don't you want to go through the test again?" I asked.

"Just the application questions."

I gave him the test, and he got all the answers right.

"You've been waiting for your citizenship for thirteen years," I said. "I've been waiting ten years since I lost my agent to meet the right agent and publisher."

"You had an agent before?"

"Yes, I told you about her. The big New York agent."

"That lady that made two people cry at the conference?"

"Yes, she was my agent. Who did you think she was?"

He said nothing, and I opened the school's third-quarter study guide and read:

> This third-quarter is like a knot-hole. It can be a tight squeeze bringing up uncomfortable feelings, emotions, and thoughts. You cannot carry old negative thoughts and ideas about yourself through this knot-hole. We often hold ourselves back because we cannot forgive ourselves or others for being human. Forgiveness is an incredibly powerful tool. Use your tools…If you are not feeling heard in the world or within your work, why? Who do you need to forgive?

I turned off the light and leaned close to my husband. He called me crazy, turned around, and embraced me wholeheartedly, telling me how much he loved me and how much I meant to him. I realized, I love being a housewife. Yes, once in a while my spirit is tempted to fly. It kicks here and there, but then it comes to its senses and remembers its priority and is happy to come home. My love for my home, my desire to attend to my family's needs, has caused me to trim all the unwanted fat off my life. It forced me to walk a tight rope, and that was a good thing. But it also felt sad. It saddened me to let go of that drama, to watch a situation as an observer and not a participant.

"There's sadness because what has connected you to the people no longer exists," Fiona said after I expressed how I'd been feeling lately. "They may not need you anymore."

"Over the years, I've known this is not where I want to be, but I always fell into the drama in order to please others on the outside."

"You pleased the outside and ignored the inside. Now you realize that by ignoring the inside, you are not really serving anyone. If I was a mess, I wouldn't be able to help you. When people see that you are happy, they can't be anything outside of that too. You have to raise yourself up to be able to help others. People in the school have to even raise themselves up or drop out. And they'll use every excuse they want, but it's them not rising up to the energy."

My daughter barged in. "Mom, I want yellow rice."

"Shhh!" I placed my finger over my mouth.

Using huge gestures, she silently said the same thing. I went into the living room, which was so loud because of the sitcoms she was watching. My son started jumping on the chair, saying...I couldn't comprehend what. I tried to quiet him too. I put a bowl of rice in the microwave and now I could barely hear what Fiona was saying.

"Are you doing something right now?" she asked.

"I'm heating food for the kids."

Once the food was ready, I quickly returned to the bedroom.

"If you record our conversations over all this time, you'll find there's repetition most of the time. But then you chose your issues, whether consciously or not consciously – it was actually unconsciously, but you were working toward it. The unconsciousness bubbled up to the top, and you became conscious because you became aware of what you're doing. You're still looking through the old lens of how everyone was connected to you because of how you moved. And right now, you don't know how the sand will move. It might be a far more beautiful castle than it was before."

"I wouldn't be surprised. Many things change to the better when you let them be," I said. "I am no longer that same person and cannot react the way I once used to, through guilt."

"You know you don't want to move into the world through guilt because it was pulling you forward into the drama. Now you're standing straighter and your light is beginning to shine because you're becoming you. Let the glue, the sadness, the string of fibers making up the guilt melt away. Envision it chipping off, envision yourself without the sadness. I'm happy that you're recognizing this sadness. You would have nothing to recognize four weeks ago. This sadness might even be another layer of something else and not guilt. Just watch it and don't put a story on it yet."

"I guess I must own my story and let go of trying to bring other people's stories forward."

"And remember, you don't know the outcome of this. Because there's now a space in the relationship between you and others, it may grow – whether it be in one day, one year, five years, or in another lifetime. We get trapped in time because we think there's only now. But that's a huge topic we won't go into. Our vision is only seeing the immediate outcome."

"Yes, it's easier to just say screw it."

"Whenever you say that, stop and get whatever got screwed into you unscrewed."

I laughed. "Sometimes in my excitement, I want people to join me on this wonderful ride. But I see that I have to discern between meddling and actually responding. I must respect peoples' issues and let it be. It's realizing that I'm not being heartless; it's that I'm respecting it."

"You're completely honoring it. If you're holding onto it then it can't transform. If you unattach it or unscrew it, that little thing might become something else. Honor the guilt because it did its job and you're allowing it to go with someone else who needs this guilt. You may at some time in life pick it up again and let it go again. Because you've honored it, so it respects you. Now you have a relationship."

"You made me see the word guilt in a whole new light."

"Guilt is not a negative word. It's just an energy."

Chapter 19
HEALING THE SOLAR PLEXUS

In a blog post titled "The Myth of First Time Directors," David Christopher Loya talks about how studios tell filmmakers that there's no way their project will be funded unless a "known" director is attached to it. This is not true, he says, citing several people who did a hell of a job directing their first feature film and making millions, even billions of dollars doing so. They include Orson Welles, John Singleton, Quentin Tarantino, David Fincher, and many others. The author notes that "an experienced first-time feature film director is in fact one of the best bets an investor or studio can make. You will cost less, and because your focus is on the best interests of the film, you're not likely to indulge your ego at the expense of the movie."

Reading this opened a window to a dream I had closed off last year after going to Washington, DC and meeting with the Iraqi cultural attaché in the hopes of finding support for my film project. The meeting was a flop, and it made me realize that in order for me to move forward, I had to temporarily close the window to that dream. This blog post caused me to open the window and peek ever so slightly, but that little glimpse was enough to rejuvenate the desire to make my film.

During our next conversation, I told Fiona, "I want to raise my storytelling abilities from book form to the screen. I don't know how I can do that in a male-dominated industry when

I've never directed anything big before."

"You need to talk to Lynn Andrews," she said. "Her ex-husband was a producer of a major film company and she worked in it too."

I had no idea. Lynn never really brought up her personal life unless it pertained to a lesson she was trying to convey. She focused on the teachings and on helping her apprentices with questions they had. When I read her books, I sometimes wished I could see how she incorporated the Sisterhood of the Shields teachings into her modern everyday life.

Fiona advised that before my phone session with Lynn, I make a list of what I wanted to talk to Lynn about and put it on the Sacred Wheel. I said I would do that, and we soon ended our call. There was a full moon in the sky, a time to release what no longer served me. After I bathed the kids, I told them they had to stay in bed and went into the kitchen to prepare my husband's dinner of fried beef and tomatoes. Then I went into my room and closed the door. I lit a stick of incense and a scented candle, turned off all the lights, and went beneath the covers. There I centered myself and released into the hands of the universe my career struggles. I gave thanks for the experience, said good-bye, and soon became very drowsy, feeling as if my body was traveling to different parts of the world, moving from an arid desert to a mountain range, to tropical landscapes, then urban landscapes.

That night, I dreamt I was tired of being single and wanted to finally get married. I woke up the next morning and realized I am already married. This dream was a desire that represented what I was looking for in regards to my work, a true and sacred union. I needed to marry my success rather than chase after it. This would eventually lead to financial independence, which in turn would allow me to bring my mom to live with me. The other day she had called me and, with a quivering voice, said, "Don't feel bad when I die. Everyone is bound to die."

Given my mother's history, this stunt in many ways resembled the type of stunts done by the character Fred Sanford in the TV sitcom *Sanford and Son*. Fred, whenever someone agitated him or things did not go his way, would try to drag his adult son through a guilt trip by placing his hand on his chest and, pretending he was having a heart attack, speak to heaven, addressing his deceased wife. "Elizabeth, I'm coming to join you!"

Although I sensed the games my mother played in an attempt to get our attention, I also heard whispers of fear. She feared death, especially dying alone, and she wanted someone to rescue her from having to do so. The agony of her departing from this earth with a deep emptiness, despite being surrounded by her tribe of children and grandchildren, was too much for me to bear.

That week, I asked Fiona if she could help me make the list of questions for Lynn because my writing, the school, the kids, and the responsibilities around the house made it impossible for me to think straight.

"What are you afraid of?" she asked.

Ah, my least favorite question! Am I going to work on my fears for a whole lifetime and perhaps, possibly, in the next lifetime? If working to become a surgeon, I would have graduated by now. By what scientific technique did one even find these creatures called fears that were hidden in our souls like pebbles at the bottom of an ocean? A mass of annoyance consumed me because I did not want to say it.

"I have given to my writing for over twenty years," I said. "I sense the direction is now shifting. Soon I will be at the receiving end, and I'm afraid that when I'm there, I won't know how to take what I deserve."

"It's only natural that you have fear around it because it's new," she said. "It's a new place for you to express yourself, and you want to be heard. Writing is one of the most important things, but we in the Western culture don't really value it. I don't know how it is with the Eastern culture, but it's the same with nursing. If Western society really paid a nurse for what they did than the US would be bankrupt." She was silent momentarily, then said, "There's hundreds and hundreds and hundreds of thousands of books out there, and I'm not sure that the authors of these books really make money from them."

"I've worked so hard, for decades, to get where I'm at, to write full-time. If my book does not move forward, I might have to go backward, get an odd job." I added, as if to myself. "My husband's comment about my work doesn't help. He said something the other day that really upset me. The strange thing is that when we were courting, he was incredibly impressed that I wrote books. He'd said, 'Wow, you write? Writers can change people. They can change the world.'"

"Yup," she said.

"Now he's like, 'maybe you need to get a job.' Up until recently, I had been working. I found whatever jobs available that enabled me to mostly stay home and raise my kids so that I'm not working just to pay someone else to raise them. My husband and I had agreed that this type of parenting costs less and is more ideal than childcare. Besides, I work so hard in the house. I do a lot! I do a lot!"

"I know you do."

"Today it was one thing to the next," I said, unable to hold back tears. "Wrote my chapter in the morning, took my son to school, wrote at the library, came home for a bite to eat, and took the kids to the gym. My daughter had rock-climbing class. I came home and mowed the lawn, cleaned the house, kicked the kids out of the family room so I can watch TV while I cook dinner for my husband. I said to them, 'I'm stuck at the sink washing dishes, yet you, who have an iPad, iPod, computers, and TVs in your rooms must use this TV as well?' I was so angry that they scampered out of sight. I did the dishes, finished cooking dinner for my husband, and prepared a pot of curry for tomorrow's lunch, only to find that I ran out of vinegar for the curry. I substituted it with fresh dill, and then went on to do more dishes. When my daughter came out, she said, 'You're still washing dishes?' I said, 'These are new dishes from the dinner I just made.' At 10 pm, I went into the bathtub and washed my body. It was all I could do before calling you at 10:08 pm. I'm exhausted. Really, really exhausted."

"When your husband said whatever he said to you, how did it make you feel?" she asked.

"Useless."

"Knowing that he is a reflection of you, of these words, ask yourself how do I make myself useless?"

"By doing and doing and doing and doing and not rewarding myself."

"I want you to close your eyes and tell me, can you feel that in your body, and if you do, where is it?"

"It's in my stomach."

"What do you see in your stomach?"

"I see my mom."

"What's your mom doing in there?"

Crying hard, I started babbling. She could not understand

what I was saying, so she asked me to repeat it.

"She's telling me I don't know how to do anything," I said.

"Ask the little girl what she wants to do about this."

"She's not a little girl. She's twenty-something."

"Can you have a dialogue with your mom? Tell her how you feel."

"I feel like you don't see all that I am, all that I can do and all that I can be. And I don't understand why you can't see it, but I can."

"Tell her the things you can do, as if talking to her."

"I can manage a home and a business. For years I managed my brothers' video store. I babysat and tutored my nieces and nephews. I can read and write and get degrees and awards. I can cook and clean and take care of children and elders."

"What does she want you to do with this?"

"She wants me to forget about what she said in the past. It's not who she is anymore."

"Ask the twenty year old what she wants to do about it."

"I want to bury it."

"I want you to put your hand into your stomach and bring that energy out. Place it in a bundle. Take it outside, with your mother beside you, maybe even your husband, and find a spot to bury it." She gave me a moment to feel around for that energy. I saw a large chain, the kind used to detain slaves, being pulled from inside my body. "Have you found the right spot for it?"

"The area where I'd placed my power mask overnight."

"Put the energy of your mom's words in that hole and allow the earth to transform it, for Mother Earth to dissolve it and make it into something beautiful. Now envision light coming into that spot and into your mother and into your husband and into you – beautiful, loving light."

I was quiet, feeling the light in the midst of the night.

"How do you feel? Tired? Light?"

"Both."

"Things will change from now on with regards to this subject. You will either come to different terms with your work, not care what anyone says, or not do so much."

I was still and quiet, the feeling of love sustaining me.

"Is everything cleared in your solar plexus?" she asked. "No fibers are there?"

"No fibers. It's clear."

This meditation reminded me of the time she had me look at the woman I was in my early twenties, walking in the mall with my shopping bags.

"You are a goddess," I said to her.

She laughed. "You gave me goose bumps."

"It's true. To have done what you just did."

"You're doing the work."

"You also. I know what I see, and you are a goddess."

When we finished our conversation, I went into the living room and said to my son, "I'm sorry for yelling at you earlier."

"And holding a knife and following me," he said.

I laughed. "It was a butter knife."

Chapter 20
PHONE SESSION WITH LYNN

Lynn's spirit made itself present even before our scheduled phone session at 2 pm. I could not see or hear her or anything like that but felt nervous knowing she could and would disrobe my character in order to examine the wounds in my soul. She had a clever way of holding a mirror which, upon seeing yourself too clearly, makes you feel out of breath and causes the box that you've built to protect yourself fall apart. You later learn that this allows for the opportunity to open up your womb of creativity. You become impregnated with the mystery that connects everyone to the Great Spirit, where the source of our dreams lies.

I sat on the porch steps staring at the trees, a notebook, iPhone, and pen stacked on my lap. I was home alone, my daughter still at school and my son at my sister's house. The silver firs of the evergreens were still and lit brightly under the vibrant sun. No bird or squirrel or any other animal appeared to shake their calm branches. Autumn had made its camp here, coloring the tree leaves scarlet and gold. Several bees came and buzzed nearby. I realized this has become a great place of power for me, a place of importance, a place of prayer.

The time was 1:57 pm, and I hoped that the neighbor's loud lawnmower muffler, which had suddenly become noticeable, would stop before I called Lynn in a few minutes. I trusted this conversation would give me the answers I was looking for, although a part of me did not feel comfortable with that idea. Lynn had often told her apprentices that we must face and become our own power, not to wait for someone else to fill us with it. When will I arrive to that place where I could trust my own power, I wondered, as I dialed Lynn's number.

The lawnmower stopped just before Lynn answered the phone. "Who is this?"

"Weam."

"LeAnn?"

"No, Weam with a W."

"Oh sorry, Weam. I didn't recognize your voice."

I smiled.

"So, my dear, what are you calling me about?" she asked. "How can I help you?"

I told her that Fiona suggested I call her after she found out I wanted to direct films.

"People will never let a writer direct a first film," she said.

Not the words of encouragement I'd hoped to hear, but I did not plan to surrender easily. Last time she did this, last time she tested me, I caved in like a coward.

"It has happened before and it does happen and it's really not a big deal. It's not rocket science to direct a film," I said, quoting Woody Allen's words in a documentary about his life. "Plus there are no Iraqi-American directors in Hollywood, so how would they relay the story accurately?"

We went back and forth about this subject for a while because she was confusing my manuscript with the feature script. At the end of last year, and with the help of my first-year mentor, I had decided to put the feature script aside so I could focus on one project at a time. I even did ceremony to release it by burning a hard copy of it into the fireplace.

"The book and the script are two different projects," I said.

"I'm not sure what you're asking from me," she said.

We hadn't been on the phone for five minutes and, in that short amount of time, she had already pushed me off my box of security and into a prism of confusion. It felt like my mind was flashing idiocies and she, in return, was grasping these idiocies and sparkling more light upon them. I got off the porch steps and paced in the backyard, looking within for the right words to express what I really wanted.

"People normally take advantage of my abilities," I said, walking around the swing set. "I want to be in power when the right opportunity comes, whether regarding the book or the feature script, so that I'm no longer taken advantage of."

"Well, your agent should be the one telling you about this," she said.

I wished to inform her that my agent was in and out of hospitals, but I said, "She's interested in the book. The script just came about as she and I were talking."

"Tell me what your book is about."

"It's about my Iraqi-American experience, intertwined with this American girl who is of Iraqi decent. She's in prison right now."

I told her everything, how Dawn Hanna's family approached me to write a book about their daughter who was in prison, accused of conspiring with a man to deliver telecom equipment to Iraq during the UN-imposed embargo. After her sentencing, the man she was accused of conspiring with came out and declared that he is a CIA-operative and that this was a US-sponsored operation. The telecom was intended to listen in on Saddam and his men. He and another man said that Dawn knew nothing of the real destination because the project was top secret.

"What genre is it?" Lynn asked.

"It's memoir. Initially I wanted it to be less personal. I shied away from having myself in it, but the editors found it difficult to connect to the story through third person, through Dawn. They felt that the story would be more powerful and serve a greater purpose if I wrote it as a memoir. They, and the school, helped me effectively bring out the *I* in my voice."

A silence as thick as sugar syrup followed and consumed the chatter in my mind. She was grilling me, and I felt powerful in my sense of intuition and by looking within.

"It sounds wonderful, but people are going to have to read it and it must get out there and be successful in order that a film be made about it," she said.

"No, this is not the same story." I stepped into the house and peeked at the clock on the wall. Fifteen minutes had passed since I called her. I hoped we wouldn't continue in circles for the next forty-five minutes. "You know, I think I'm not really in a position to go anywhere with my feature script until I have the book out. After the book comes out, then I can ask for directing title."

"So what do you need from me? How can I help?"

"I want advice on how to be strong through the business process of the publishing industry. I want to own what is coming to me."

"It's your property, and you know that."

Property? My book was an asset of some sort?

"You might want to get a film agent, separate from the book agent," she said.

"You think I need that?"

"Yes, you need to have an agent who knows the film business, bigger agencies that are connected to the big studios."

"Maybe what I need to do before I give attention to anything else is finish the book."

"That's a really good idea. If you have trouble with the book, which it doesn't seem you will, you can also look for an agent on the side for your script. You can't really present the script until you have an agent. You have to have somebody that will sell you and sell your project. Someone has to believe enough in you to do that."

"Yeah," I said dully.

There was a long pause.

"Where's your doubt?" she asked, her voice changing since she'd caught the slippery heart of the issue.

"When you said someone has to believe enough in me, the first thought that went through my head is that I have to first believe enough in myself. I'm afraid that when the time comes to deal with people in the film or publishing industry, they will see through my doubts and will take advantage of the situation or I will sabotage it. The past rejections I dealt with have really hurt me. I've healed much of it by bouncing back on my feet and writing another book, but it has still not seen full execution, and with the film…I'm just starting out."

"You're going to have to realize that people will reject the script a million times before they accept it."

That took away all the misconceptions I had about my journey.

"Or you might get lucky and someone will pick it up from the start," she said. "Meanwhile, you need to concentrate on one thing and get it done. Period! Then get your book out and start work on the film."

"Yes, at least I already have a clear vision of where that's going."

"You will get it done. You're going to be fine. It's a lot to get a book out there."

"How long did it take you to get your book out?"

She laughed. "Oh, years! People didn't want to publish it, but then once it got published things began moving smoothly. You need to get your book published so that you've done something that somebody can point to. You need to stay focused on one project and just get it done. You need to have faith in it and see it being strong and wonderful. I think you have a fabulous project. I wouldn't blur it with other projects. And if you can, stop worrying about it. Just do it. If God wants to help you, He wouldn't know what to do. You're kind of all over the place."

Her preciseness and honesty tasted like sugar cookies. They were sweet and light and yet extremely important. They helped me see why I kept hitting a slump.

"Stick with that, with the book. Do it! Live it! You're really onto something wonderful. If you were speaking to God, what would you tell him you want? Tell God what you want!"

"I want to write a great book and have it be successful in the publishing industry."

"Well, you've already written the book, haven't you?"

Two truths I discovered in less than an hour: I owned creative property and I've already written the book. Suddenly I felt a concrete fortress of support.

"Then say, 'I've written a book and now I need to make sure that it gets published properly,'" she said. "You need to set it free. I'm going to have you do something. Make a medicine bundle from red material. Tie feathers to it, and then you need something from all the people who have had something to do with this book – piece of hair or blood, something personal. Put it in the bundle, all right?"

"Okay."

"Oh, and write a prayer to the Great Spirit in the bundle. Place all those pieces into the medicine bundle. And you wrap it up with feathers and put steamers around it with the colors of the four directions. Do you know the colors for the four directions?"

"No."

"What year are you?"

"Second."

"Second, and you don't know the colors of the directions? Oh my God!"

She described the colors: East (gold), North (yellow), West (black), South (red).

"Then you take those and find a tree or a branch," she continued. "Find a place where you absolutely know someone will pick it up and what they do with it does not matter. And ask the Great Spirit to help you send this book to its very highest good. Okay?"

"Yes."

"Comprende, my darling? Do you see what I'm saying?"

"Yes."

"Good. I just want you to feel strong about this. It will be fine, okay? And you send it on its way, to its highest good, and let it go. And you have to have a little thing from you, some kind of special prayer. Once you let it go to its highest good, you have your agent doing the work on it." She paused. "Does that help you?"

"Yes."

"Perfect." She laughed. "Well, I'm thrilled. You know lots

of things will come up and you will not know what to do. That's when you'll call me."

"I don't think I'll call you about this anymore although I will call you about other things. I love talking to you."

She laughed. "You are so cute. I think you're going to do great things. When you do something creative like this, it is also spiritual. Do you understand that?"

"Yes. Since my late teens, early twenties, I've cared about three things: family, writing, and service. I wasn't sure how I can serve through my writing but that has become clear to me over the past few years, and especially after I began reading your books. Your books and school have done so much for people, women in particular. I'm writing my own experience with the school and that's going to be my next book."

"It is?"

"Yes. I hope to be able to inspire women to find an ancient, healthy outlet for themselves. I've seen what some wrote about you online, of people accusing you of brainwashing the women. Well, we've never even met in person and yet your teachings have helped change my life. What I read in your books, what you teach in the school, I'm more familiar with that than the modern Western world. To me, that's more normal and it was a normal part of my ancestors."

"Who are your ancestors?"

"They're the Chaldeans, from land of the Chaldeas, where Prophet Abraham was born. The first writer in recorded history is Enheduanna, a woman from Mesopotamia, ancient Iraq. Thousands of years ago, my people were involved in the things you write about, that's still part of your teachers' lives – the magic and sorcery."

"You were born in Baghdad?"

"Yes."

"This life that you're talking about was part of the ancient cities of Persia and Iraq is so far away from what it is like now. I have five or six pots that are over five thousand years old from that part of the world."

"Really?"

"They are beautiful. So much has been destroyed now by Muslim fundamentalists."

We were quiet, adorned by oneness in admiration for that land. She had expressed herself with a paint brush that changed the color of my doubt from dark to light. By honoring my birthplace, she honored me, nudging me forward into a den of diamonds I feared to enter into for lack of self-worth.

I reminded her that our time was nearly up, but she did not let me go, and we continued to chit-chat. I told her that our talk had really helped.

"You've inspired me too because I'm so drawn to that world, the Bedouins," she said. "They raised the true Arabian horses, you know. It's fascinating. But the fundamentalists are destroying all that too."

At 3:15 pm, she pulled herself from the conversation. She said she'd better close our session, said a prayer, and said, "Okay, dear, Namaste."

I felt exhausted and exhilarated after I finished talking to Lynn. The energy fibers she streaks over your chakras manipulates your negativities into positivities. You then have no choice but to shift, to grow.

Slowly, I walked to my mailbox and when I opened it, I found a letter for my husband. His naturalization ceremony was next Thursday, October 3, at 9:30 am. I called him at once and, smiling wide, asked, "If I give you good news, what will you give me?"

"Anything you want."

"California," I said, feeling that finally I would make it to Storm Eagle.

"Okay, but I will come."

"What about the kids? I feel bad to leave them alone."

"We'll take them with us."

How realistic is that?

I told Fiona about my conversation with Lynn, how in the beginning of our conversation, I had thought, "This is going nowhere!" Lynn kept saying, "I don't understand exactly why you called me, how you want me to help." I explained again and again. She would act confused and say, "But what is it that you want?" I would again explain, more clearly, and she would again act like she was at a loss, all the meanwhile my eye on the clock, thinking, "Half of our call is over and we haven't gotten anywhere!"

As I continued with Fiona, I opened the bathroom door to see what my son was doing. He stood at the sink, scooping Vaseline out of a large container and mixing it with toothpaste into a blue plastic cup. Then he added water. As he glanced at me from the side, knowing I was angry but busy on the phone, he stirred his concoction, which was spilling over the sink and onto the floor because the faucet was running.

My nerves shot up, but I just could not do anything about it. I stepped out of the bathroom, deciding to let my husband handle this when he came home, and continued to tell Fiona how Lynn eventually helped me bring the boat to shore, that she was messing around with me, like her teachers messed around with her, to get me to focus on and be specific about what I wanted.

It worked. She moved me out of the circle of work and into the vision of the next phase of my career. The part that surprised me was when the clock ticked at the end of the hour and she kept wanting to talk to me, unlike the last two conversations, where she'd ended the call promptly.

"When I hung up, I was excited and exhausted," I said. "I wanted to sleep, but I had to pick up my son from my sister's house. When my sister was talking to me, I was not really there but an observer. I was out of my body and I thought, does my sister even know that I'm not here?"

Fiona laughed. "What you experienced that day is multiplied a gazillion times at Storm Eagle."

"I prayed a lot about Storm Eagle, but I haven't received the push I need. My husband does not like that I would take another trip without him, another 'vacation,' where he would have to take time off of work to watch the kids."

"Can one of your sisters or your mother help?"

"My mother these days is the one needing help, and all my sisters work. My son is very attached to me, so it's important that my husband is there."

"Maybe this has to do with what your talk with Lynn was about."

"What?"

"Being specific about what you want."

"I did that initially, but if my husband's attitude has not changed toward it, what can I do? I don't want to be aggressive and put a wedge between us when we have been on good terms for so long. Since last week, for instance, he has helped me around the house on several occasions without me asking him to."

"I want you to create with your clay a power object, putting everything in it to get you there. Call your concerns that you have about coming. Then make a wedge of another clay, or a piece of anything that is a little sharp, and slice the first object in half. Then create something that will help you get there."

My husband returned home and cleaned my son and the mess that he had made in the bathroom. I looked within about creating a power object with clay. Something about it did not feel right. I wanted my husband to agree without any coercion so that the trip would go smooth and be blessed, so I skipped it.

Chapter 21

THE NATURALIZATION CEREMONY

The alarm clock went off at 7:30 am. I could barely get out of bed, but my husband hurried to my daughter's room to wake her up. He told her she would not be going to school today, and I heard her ask all sorts of questions. I allowed my son to sleep as I got ready and tried not to forget anything: the cell phones, camera, and GPS I had charged last night, the MapQuest directions, snacks for the kids and their backpacks in case there was time to drop them off to school after our 9:30 am appointment. I asked my daughter what class she had today. "Gym," she said.

"Then wear your jogging suit and gym shoes."

We were dressed and out of the house by 8:15 am. The drive downtown was smooth although my husband complained about the traffic. I could tell by the number of times he'd kissed the rosary hanging on the rear view mirror and then crossed himself that he was nervous.

"The GPS and MapQuest are giving us two different directions," I said. "Which one should we follow?"

"MapQuest."

Shortly afterward he missed Exit 50, Grand River Avenue.

"That's the exit you were supposed to take," I said, trying not to snap. "Okay, then take Lafayette Boulevard."

He again kissed the rosary and crossed himself.

"Mommy, my tummy hurts," my son cried.

"We're almost there, *habbibi*." I turned to my husband. "Did you take him to the bathroom?"

"No, I changed him while he was still sleeping and carried him to the car."

We were on the highway, so I had to think quickly. I looked at the coffee cups and, remembering that one of my friends had her son pee in two-liter Coke bottles when he was potty training, decided that if the situation required it, I'd have my son pee in one of the cups. Then I looked at the GPS and told my husband to stay on the right side and get off at the next exit. He decided to follow a different direction and passed the exit, causing the GPS to change the distance time from 2:06 minutes to 9:12 minutes.

I still tried not to snap. "What are you doing?"

We both glanced at the clock. It was 9:10 am and our court proceeding was at 9:30 am.

"It'll be fine," he said, taking out his cigarillo, a short and narrow cigar that he began to use after he quit smoking cigarettes. They were supposed to be an alternative to cigarettes although a cigarillo contains about three grams of tobacco and a cigarette contains less than one gram. He reasoned that since he only took a few puffs a day of the cigarillo and mostly during cases of real frustrations, like in this moment, it was not as bad.

"Are we in Chinatown?" my daughter asked. We didn't answer. "We are in Chinatown, I know it!"

"Yeah, this looks like Chinatown," my son said. "I don't want to go to China. I hate Indian food."

She kept going with the Chinatown thing and suddenly, we realized she had my iPhone and had called my cousin to tell her we were in Chinatown. I demanded she give me the phone. My husband was oh so upset. He didn't want to tell anyone we were going to the courthouse so they would not jinx it. I hung up the phone, and when my cousin continuously rang to see if we were okay, I did not pick up. I sent her a text message that I was busy in an appointment.

My son persisted about his tummy ache, even as we waited in the long line into the Detroit Federal Building. I was concerned that he would not be able to hold it and prayed all would be fine, that no one would throw up or have other types of accidents, until the naturalization ceremony was over with. We had waited nine years after we got married for this day to come. My husband had been waiting for thirteen years, if we were to count from the time he left Iraq.

I took my children to the restroom while my husband went into the courtroom to reserve seats for us. When I returned, I saw he was sitting toward the back.

"No, I want to sit in the front," I said.

We moved to the first row. I put my stuff on the chairs and then took my son out of the courtroom and into a little snack store in the building. I noticed there was no register. At the register-less counter, a middle-aged man with an apron came up and asked, "What do you have?"

I realized he was blind. "A bag of Famous Amos chocolate chip cookies and a large coffee."

No food or drink was allowed inside the courtroom, so my son and I sat on the wooden sofa in the hallway. On the wall behind the sofa was a large handwritten copy of the Declaration of Independence, the Bill of Rights and the Constitution. "We the People," I read and thought about the words of Ron Paul, about whistleblower Edward Snowden who, in June 2013, took refuge in Hong Kong. "We live in a bad time where American citizens don't even have rights and can be killed as a result," he said. "It's a shame that we are in an age where people who tell the truth about what the government is doing get into trouble. What about the people who destroy our Constitution?"

As I fed my son cookies and drank my coffee, I read bits of pieces of the law documents on the wall, even though they were hard to make out in cursive.

"Mommy, can we get that?" my son asked, pointing to the large American flag hanging from the ceiling.

I looked up and stared at the colorful fabric, remembering the flag Linda, Dawn Hanna's mother, had taken down. "It is beautiful, isn't it?"

"Yeah!" he said.

I returned my son inside the courtroom. Because I'd only had a few sips of my coffee and the ceremony was not going to start for another half an hour, I took a stroll in the hallway. There was a plaque beside the courtroom stating that the building was erected in 1934 under the Herbert Hoover administration. A wall near the security entrance had pictures of each US president, beneath him a memorable quote. The words of President George Bush Sr. were the most interesting. In his speech to a session of the Supreme Soviet of Ukraine, on August 1, 1991, he said, "When Americans talk of freedom, we refer to peoples' abilities to live without fear of government intrusion, without fear of their fellow citizens, without harassment by restricting others' freedoms. We do not consider freedom a privilege to be doled out only to those who hold proper political views or belong to a certain group."

The ceremony began promptly at 10:30 am.

"We know that for most of you, this has been a long journey across many lands," said the Hispanic immigration officer at the podium. "Let's give a round of applause for yourselves and each other."

Everyone clapped. My son, in his excitement, pushed for the umpteenth time his chair against the lady behind us, hitting her feet. This time she cried in pain. I apologized and had my son do the same. The immigration officer continued with his speech and, in the end, asked if we had any questions. My son raised his hand. "I do." A few people behind us laughed. Because he was not called upon, he grabbed my left arm by my jacket and lifted it up. The officer said, "Yes, ma'am, you have a question?"

"Sorry, my son did that."

The judge soon took the stage. She was a thin woman with a long face and straight, thin hair. She congratulated everyone on this day, commenting that despite a government shutdown in the city of Detroit, we were all here.

"This is a great country, but it is not perfect," she said. "But hopefully, we persevere and stay united."

The judge talked about how this country had a rich history of welcoming immigrants and told us her personal story. Her parents came to this country from Russia. She was born here, and what she noticed was that those born here sometimes forgot just how important the Constitution is. "The right to practice your own religion, the right to speak freely, and the right to pursue your own version of happiness, not someone else's dream," she said. "I just want to say that when you exercise the right to criticize, to also offer a solution. Utilize the knowledge, experiences, and talents you brought from another land to help with the challenges we have in this land. Citizenship is not only a new set of status. It is also a set of responsibilities."

I was incredibly moved. I thought of the words I lived by:

family, writing, service. I also remembered one thing my mother often said. "Oh, if I only knew how to read and write, the things I could have done." My father's love for books, my love for family and culture, and my mother's unfulfilled desires to read and write were what kept me wide-eyed and alert to the responsibility of my career. They were the reasons I had agreed to write the Dawn Hanna story.

It was time to play the Star Spangled Banner. We all stood and faced the flag mounted on the stage like an Akkadian princess with wings. We placed our right hand on our heart area. The judge held an iPad against the microphone and suddenly the vigorous and flawless voice of Whitney Houston stirred the courtroom with emotions of joy, triumphs, appreciation, but also sadness. Tears welled through my whole body as I thought of my ancestors and their struggles to leave an oppressive regime to come to this country and experience freedom. The sacrifices they made, the blood they shed.

The last time I attended a naturalization ceremony was over fifteen years ago, when my mother became a citizen. My mother never went to school, she never learned the alphabet, and she never held a job. The only accomplishment she achieved outside of raising twelve children and keeping a good home was the attainment of her US Citizenship, and she got it because she wanted to be an American, like all her children. The energy of my parents and their descendants, the ancient Mesopotamian civilizations who were the first to record their thoughts in writing and whose ancestry traces back to Ur of the Chaldea, the birthplace of Abraham, were in that courtroom with us.

They began calling the names of the eighty-plus men and women who were naturalized. At the end, they asked the children who did not go to school today to come up on stage and do the Pledge of Allegiance. One middle aged black man from Cameroon in Africa interrupted, saying, "My name was not called." There was a very worried expression on his face. The judge stopped everything and asked a young lady who was sent to the ceremony on behalf of Governor Rick Snyder's office to look into the matter. We waited until his naturalization certificate was found. Everyone cheered and clapped. On the way out of the courtroom, we saw the wife of the African man pat his bald head with a large white napkin as he stood there sweating and smiling with embarrassment. I could not help but laugh.

"I don't blame him for getting so scared," my husband said. "If that was me, I would have had a heart attack. Since that day I spent in prison, I have not had one good night's sleep."

Neither had I.

He inhaled deeply. "Now I can breathe." He turned to me. "I got this through you, *habbibi*. Thank you."

I was thankful, too. This process had made me feel un-American. Yet it also strengthened my American values.

Chapter 22
MAKING A BUNDLE

"I'm going outside for a minute," I told my husband after he ordered a smoothie.

We were on a date night at Partridge Creek Mall, which my children and I call The Doggy Mall because many people bring their dogs, some all decked-out as if going to a fancy dress ball, and parade them around. Unbeknownst to my husband, I chose this place to release my bundle.

I stepped out of Surf City Squeeze and looked around the outdoor mall. The lit up storefronts, trees, and flowers decorated with Christmas lights made the area look like a capturing painting that one wished to step and disappear into. I placed the bundle that Lynn suggested I make into a bush of flowers, red and purple chrysanthemums. After saying a little prayer, I let the bundle go and sat on the bench, allowing the power of the clear night sky and the cool October breeze to surround me like a devotional parasol.

"Where did you go?" my husband asked.

I turned toward him, staring into those eyes which always loved me even when the brows were knitted by raging emotions. "Just wanted to sit here and observe the beautiful scenery."

That night I dreamt I was with my family at a banquet center. I had to recite poetry wearing a dress that was on top of this other dress. I went into the ladies' room and removed the upper dress. I felt so much lighter. Underneath was a floral dress and over it a dark green shawl. I fixed the shawl so that it would not fall off and returned to my table, where my sister told me she had a gift for me. She proudly put a long gold chain around my neck and said, "My daughter picked it out for you."

I held the charms and observed them closely; one had a cross/sword-like shape, and the other was the palm of a hand, to ward off evil spirits.

"This is just like my daughter's hand palm necklace," I said.

We returned to the banquet center and stood at a food station that served wrapped salads and unique breads. I made myself a plate and returned to my table. The show began, and I suddenly realized I had no makeup on and should wear some. I rushed to the ladies' room and, while standing in front of the mirror, decided to remove the shawl. I felt much lighter and looked slimmer. I wondered, why did I have all these layers on?

That next morning I finished the manuscript and went outside for a breath of fresh air. Reflecting on the depth, humor, pain, and meaning that turned my life into love incense, I took several deep grateful breaths and sighs. A black and brown squirrel vivaciously chased each other across the lawn. They hopped on a tree trunk and spun around it several times, their tails moving like a fast paint brush expressing itself on canvas. Finally they made it to the top, causing the tree branches to shake and a few leaves to drop to the ground.

I returned inside the house and packed a lunch for my daughter. After my husband left to take her to school, I cuddled in bed next to my sleeping son. This time I dreamt of my mother. She was in my arms, like a baby, and I wept over her, though she was alive. Her breaths slowed down, ready to shut off. She would soon have no breaths to breathe.

The phone rang, waking me up. There were tears all over my face.

The next day my sisters and I took my mother to Bahama Breeze for one of my sister's birthdays. We sat in the covered outdoor patio, which had a fireplace. It started raining shortly after we arrived. We discussed what we planned to order.

"Mom, do you want chicken or a hamburger?" Niran asked her.

"Whatever you want," she replied.

"Mom, you're the one who is going to eat it. Which do you want?"

"Whatever you want."

It took some six times of my sister pressing for a concrete answer before my mom said, "Hamburger."

The waitress brought me my lemon ginger Mojito. I watched the mint leaves swim in my glass. The smell of the mint leaves reminded me of the olden days, of Iraqi gardens where people grew mint and dipped it in their tea or stuffed it in their sandwiches the way they did with parsley. As my sisters told stories, I kept my eyes on my drink, which was beginning to look like a river of history. I saw the painful death of my mother's first born son, George, whose loss she could never talk about. I had gathered from the tidbits of information that George, when he was a toddler, got sick after a trip she took to visit her parents' then Christian village of Telkaif. I also gathered that, initially, my father blamed her for this misfortune.

What type of fear did this incident anchor into my mother's young heart? She must have been only fourteen or fifteen years old at the time. Did the discrimination and intimidation my husband faced with the immigration department create a similar fear inside of me? Up until last week, when my husband finally received his citizenship, I felt as if someone had wrapped my body in rope and placed me on railroad tracks, where I had no other option than to await my fate. Would a train appear and destroy me by breaking apart my family, or would someone come to rescue me?

Cold air came through, and one of my sisters got up and closed the open window. As the waitress brought our plates, I remembered a school assignment I did not long ago where I realized that, on the Sacred Wheel, I was a north-east type of person, operating mostly from a spiritual and thought-provoking side. I was okay in the south, the physical plane, but I really needed to have a balance in the west, regarding my emotions. I had sadness, deep-rooted sadness, even anger, about the amount of work I had to do and my inability to ask for help. My self-sufficiency was mistaken for apathy, and as a result, I received little or no compassion from those around me.

If someone would have taken the time to ask, how do you really and truly feel, then genuinely listened to my reply without interruption of any sort, I would have said, "I feel tired." I started working when I was twelve years old. As the youngest sister, with the majority of my older siblings married by the time I was a preteen, for the next two decades I became the designated babysitter, sometimes nanny, with other tasks that got piled on along the way such as tutoring, mentoring, and providing my nieces and nephews with trips to cultural and educational places, like the library or plays. From that early age, I learned to work at my brother's party store and at my other brother's video store. Once I graduated college at age twenty-one, I became, for the most part, my mother's keeper. Since she did not have a driver's license, nor did she speak English, I drove her to her doctors' appointments, the produce market, to visit family, friends, and relatives. I played the role of a daughter, sister, and aunt as best as I could, and then I got married, and as best as I could, I played the role of a wife and mother.

Once I got married, I had to transition my energy into my home, which was not an easy transition for me since I'd lived under my mother's roof for thirty-five years. I later realized that it was also not an easy transition for my family, who were accustomed to having me belong to their needs and not swept away by a man who happened to be high maintenance, expecting me to cater to his needs most hours of the day. It was not until I learned about the different mother energies in the first year of school that I began to set boundaries and look into my own needs. In *Book 1* of this memoir series, I talked extensively about these energies, which are known in some indigenous traditions, including that of the Mayans, as *La Ultima Madre*, which translates to the Final Mother and represents Mother Earth. These energies are the Rainbow Mother and the Great Nurturing Mother.

Lynn Andrews describes the Rainbow Mother as that of the poet and dancer, a woman who wants to dream and inspire people to health and well-being, but who is completely misunderstood by a society that often sees her as eccentric. When she molds herself into peoples' definitions and expectations of her or when she abandons her dreams to gain others' approval, she then becomes her opposite energy, Crazy Woman. She may even turn to alcohol or drugs, maybe even suicide, to block or end the frustrations that stem from an unfulfilled life.

Lynn describes the Great Nurturing Mother as someone who loves routine, gets married, raises her children and is a pillar of society. But her controlling tendencies can drive her children and those around her haywire. Her opposite energy comes in during midlife, when her children are grown and there is no one left to nurture. Then she becomes Death Mother, pulling the strings of her children through guilt, depression, and death.

This did not mean that an energy was better or worse than the other. Like the yin and the yang, the feminine and the masculine, these energies are meant to complement and balance each other. To do that, a person must first understand and honor their own nature and not try to force the other person to become like them. Nor did it mean that one energy did not have any of the characteristics of the other energy. A Nurturing Mother could also love to express her creativity through poetry and painting, and a Rainbow Mother could also want to create a nurturing space for her children to come home to.

While some of the apprentices in the first year of the school had difficulty identifying which mother energies they were at the core, I recognized myself immediately. I was a Rainbow Mother and my mother was a Nurturing Mother and that was why, although we loved each other very much, our misunderstandings had prevented us from having a healthy bond. As for my Middle Eastern culture, of course they praised the Nurturing Mother and had little or no regard for the Rainbow Mother who, like many men, had dreams and aspirations outside of the home. Knowing the core of my energy freed me, because it was then that I knew I was not crazy, but that if I did not take special care of my dreams, I would become just that.

Once home, I quickly changed into my house clothes and gathered my children around the fireplace. My daughter ate the leftover jerky chicken pasta I brought from the restaurant. I had my coffee, and my son drank hot cocoa and ate pizza as he played with Batman Lego. We listened to Bible scriptures on the iPad. It felt good to be done with the manuscript for now, to just sit in peace with my children. I was grateful for my life but sad for my mother. Something about her situation did not feel right. Her glazed look and nonresponsive ways stemmed from a shock and disappointment that had settled inside of her after she'd left my brother's home and went to live with one of my sisters.

It is the custom in Arab culture for the elderly to live with one of their sons after everyone else has moved away. My mother, my then single brother, and I lived under one roof until he got married and brought his wife to live with us. For years, everyone got along great. Then I got married and my mother and my sister-in-law, both Nurturing Mothers with controlling tendencies, started to easily upset each other. The solution was pretty black and white, for my mother to move into one of her daughter's home. Of course such a simple and common-sense solution was beyond my family's routine or comprehension. Instead, we were dragged into a guilt trip that felt like the hallway entrance into the colosseum to meet the wild animal awaiting their feast. The spectacle created in our living rooms as a result fed everyone's egos, though they did not see it that way. How so? It supplied a fresh batch of drama for my siblings and demonstrated the extent of power my mother had on us.

On the way to the gym the next day, I stopped at a red traffic light near Crooks Road. A mammoth of black birds flew and landed on the trees in and around the cemetery that we passed all the time. At first glance, I felt this was a sign of flourishing. Since people viewed bird droppings as good luck, hundreds of bird droppings would be the ultimate sign of prosperity. The traffic light turned green. As my foot moved from the brakes to the gas petal, the enormous stack of black birds next to a cemetery suddenly suggested a sign opposite of flourishing. Death came to mind, along with my mother. After nearly a century of toiling over a dozen children, of investing an astronomic amount of planning her life around our lives, did she feel that we had failed her? A wave of emotional guilt struck over the guilt that I already had from before and it grew heavier by the idea that there was nothing I could do to alleviate her pain and sorrow.

* * *

I lost count of how many revisions I had made to my manuscript, but soon after I celebrated finishing what I thought was the final draft, I woke up in the middle of the night thinking, the book is not finished. Its substance was as lopsided as the Leaning Tower of Pisa. Certain chapters were simple and clear, full of depth, power, and vivid language. Other chapters were as dry as black-eyed beans. There was information in there that was like the hard skin of an onion, keeping the scent and edible portions hidden beneath the surface. I had to peel off the skin in order to let the aromas and flavors spread through the senses to create a delicious feast. How else would the reader taste my story?

I spent ample time sitting outside, staring at the evergreens, observing the spot in the earth where my daughter and I knelt over a blanket and did a ceremony to awaken my sacred mask. Four stones had circled us, one in each direction. Holding the white mask that I received in the mail from Lynn Andrews, I asked for Spirit to come in from all directions: north, south, east, and west. I listened to what was said to me before I buried, as instructed, this mask face-down into the earth. After singing my Power Song, I invited my power animal, my ancestors, the Sisterhood of the Shields, and all those who loved me as I prayed boldly and wholeheartedly to the Great Spirit.

The next day, I removed the dirt off the mask and decorated it using acrylic paint, sequins, and beads. I set the mask in my office but that spot in the earth carried a different type of energy, one which I have afterward visited whenever I needed guidance. Sitting on the porch steps, I focused on that spot and tried to discover what was missing. The manuscript. It had to be revised and sent to the editor once again, so the timing would coincide with the *Impeccability Card* from Lynn's *The Power Deck,* which encourages you to move into that place of perfection within you, to collect your discipline like a Buddha meditating and to gather your power with the intensity of a rubber band pulled and held at its breaking point.

I spent much of October rewriting and de-cluttering my home and closets. I set a day for my sisters to come over so we could make *kubba*, meat-filled dumplings. It was a school day with beautiful weather outside. As I walked my daughter to her class, I noticed large fresh sunflowers lying on the floor near the school building. Their yellow leaves had dried to a greenish color. Beside them were also garden pots filled with soil. The sunflowers must have been a school project of some sort. I picked up one of them. My daughter stared at me as I tenderly touched the seeds.

"After school, you will help me remove the seeds and then we will roast them," I said, wanting to remove whatever fears were left as a result of my husband's eight-year immigration ordeal.

I did a few errands and came home in time to prepare cardamom tea for my husband. He had already boiled eggs for breakfast and then went to buy fresh bread. I went to clean the basement, and my son followed me. He asked if he could help.

"Can you grab the golf sticks and put them against that corner?" I asked.

He frowned. "You mean the gulf clubs, Mamma?"

He had the habit of correcting anyone who did not use the proper words to describe something. Once I told him that he was hit above his eyes and he said, "Actually Mamma, it was my eyebrow."

Upstairs, my husband tried to fix the TV. Several rays of colors ran across its screen.

"It's dead," I told him. "Maybe now we can have peace and quiet in the house."

He kept trying to fix it. It got worse and worse, to where the whole screen was a blob of color. He finally left for work, and I cleaned and organized the garage. I cooked an Indian dish for when my sisters and I finished making the *kubba*.

Shortly after everyone arrived, my uncle's wife threw the sunflower seeds onto the grass, thinking they were garbage. My mother then fell to the ground on her way to the bathroom. Two of my sisters surrounded her, trying to get her up. The area became chaotic. I quickly went and had one sister hold her hands while I lifted her up from the back.

"Why are her legs so frail?" I asked.

"What do you mean?" Niran asked defensively. My mom had been staying with her. "They're always like that!"

"Not this bad. Today they're not holding up at all."

She insisted it was always like that and I said no, it was not.

"Not long ago, she spent quite a few days over my house," I said. "During that time, she was able to walk. Of course, it was with assistance. But she walked."

"Weam isn't saying anything wrong," my other sister said. "She just wants to know if there have been any major changes recently. Her legs are normally not that bad."

"Well, before we came here, her walker slipped down the ramp and she fell," she said, much calmer now and not taking things personally. "I will take her to the doctor tomorrow."

We prepared the table for the *kubba*. I glanced at my mother every so often, noticing that she was not participating with us. Once upon a time, she headed the table and gave out instructions. I was grateful that at least she saw us carrying on the tradition. After we were done, we ate dinner and then I brought out from my bedroom the bags of clothes I wanted to give away. Then I grabbed the book *Mom, Share Your Life with Me* and began asking my mom questions. One of my sisters said, "Weam is always asking Mom questions from that book of hers. But she never asks why Mom had criticized us the way she had."

"Because it was true!" my mom said, sternly but in such a cute way that we all laughed.

I walked from behind the kitchen counter and came to hug her. "I don't care about all that past," I said. "She's my mom and I love her, and I am thankful she is here."

We kissed and hugged.

"Of course, you're her little darling," my sister joked.

"I'm just happy that she's here. I don't know what will be tomorrow."

That night, I had another dream about my mom. My sisters were with her, and I was there too, but I had to leave. As I gathered my children to walk away, I said, "Come over to my house afterward." One of my sisters said, "Oh, that would be burdensome, to get Mom up, then bring her to your house." Another sister said, "No, it's not burdensome. We can do it."

My sister was holding her from the side, and my mother was leaning over like a baby without the proper strength to sit up right. She had no backbone. I rushed to my mother and hugged her, told her how much I loved her, thanked her a thousand times for all she had done for us, and apologized for all the trouble I had given her. She kissed and hugged me. I was drenched with tears. My sisters were crying, too.

I woke up, again with teary eyes, and I called my sister to ask how my mom was doing. She said, "She's not doing too good."

"Why?"

"Because of the fall she had yesterday. Her arm really hurts. She couldn't get out of bed today."

I went to bed and prayed. "Please God, when her time comes, don't let her suffer." I wanted to give her permission to go, but instead I found myself telling her to stay with us.

Chapter 23
WHATEVER

"What was your bad dream?" I asked, lying beside my daughter on her bed.

She stared at the ceiling. "An evil guy took over the earth. He stole all the colors and everything and there was no longer an earth. A king helped save the earth, but it didn't work. There was a bomb that exploded and a good guy came to try to take all the color from the evil man. The evil man put another bomb and it exploded and the good guy turned into a bad guy."

God forbid, I thought.

On the next full moon I released the pattern of obstacles regarding my work. In yoga class, when the instructor told us not to collapse, I thought, that's the answer to my nighttime troubles. Every night, by eight or nine o'clock, I would be tired and yet I had a load of work ahead of me: cleaning the house for the third or fourth time, preparing food for my husband, getting the kids ready for bed. By then, I would be hungry since I hadn't taken the time to eat dinner. I collapsed and became angry and frustrated inside because I was exhausted and there seemed to be no end in sight.

When I called Fiona, her voice was very hoarse. She was recovering from a virus that had hit her and had spent the majority of the week sleeping. Today she did not get up until 4 pm. I asked if we should postpone our session, and she said no, to tell her what was happening with me. I updated her about what had taken place in the last two weeks and that, due to family obligations, I would not make it to Storm Eagle.

"I hope you are not disappointed about that," I said.

"No, this is not about me. It's about you. This obstacle is teaching you a lot, which is perfect. Strengthening family dynamics is very important to you, and that's a beautiful thing."

"Thank you for saying that. It means a lot to me."

"I saw the Facebook post you have up of you and your sisters cooking together. It was beautiful, and for you this is very important. I do ask you that next year you do whatever you can to make it. Next year is the marriage ceremony, when you marry self-to-self, and it's an experience that will change your life. I cannot express it in words. You won't believe it, but you will believe."

The next day, on the way to pick up my daughter from school, we found a pile of acorns on the floor. They reminded me of Iraq, when we would roast them on a fire. I grabbed a handful and placed them in my son's bicycle pouch. That night, I started a fireplace and roasted them. The smell was delicious but they tasted bitter, unlike the way they tasted in Iraq. My friend Dunya Mikhail, the poet, stopped by, and when she saw the acorns she said, "That's *baloot*!"

"Is that what it's called?" I said. "I knew their smell was familiar, but I could not remember the name of this nut in Arabic."

As Iraqi-born writers and mothers who lived a mile from each other, Dunya and I shared quite a bit together. We especially loved to talk about our craft. She told me that in Iraq, she and other writers would debate that in order to be a great writer, one must suffer, be poor, not drive a nice car – opposite of Dunya's life. She disagreed. She feels writing is a luxury.

"I had read about writers turning to alcohol or drugs or living a crazy lifestyle in order to be great writers," I said. "I never agreed with that."

"Of course not! You actually need a clear mind in order to focus."

"It's a myth that a writer must be poor or an addict or suffer."

"Yes, it's a myth."

She said that for her next project her husband suggested maybe she ought to write a novel. But for her, a novel went at the same slow pace as marriage. A poem was like love, as exuberating as a climax. We laughed.

"It might then be a challenge for you to write a novel," I said. "Of course in narrative there is a lot of beauty and exhilaration, but you start a big project from scratch. It's like building a house. You design and plan. You begin to buy the equipment and tools. One by one you put up the wood and the brick. You don't get to see what you are doing until the bricks and wood are up and the rooms begin to show. Only then do you start feeling those climaxes. With you, you are the person who goes into a room that is already built and you design it. It is a quicker result."

She agreed. "I like that part that is a luxury."

I liked the word *luxury*. It kept repeating itself in my head as she told me that she was invited to China the week before Thanksgiving to lecture about poetry and globalization. Later in bed, I continued to reflect on the word *luxury* and wondered if, the economic and material aspects aside, a writer could be great, or even good, if she or he had not suffered? Although its results are not immediately visible, grief and sorrow deepen a person, makes them reflect on life, reminds them about humility and grace and kills a layer of their ego in the sweetest way, thus arousing their consciousness.

Writers who suffered as a result of having the courage to live their truths have the opportunity, through words, to slice through our differences and connect to the force which we all share. Then, within the spirit of these words, a love occurs between the writer and the reader. Through verbal silence, the writer enters the reader's soul, stills it for a long enough time for the writer to share their thoughts, feelings, and inspirations, which might serve in a way no one but the divine can imagine or understand.

* * *

Sunday the pastor baptized one of his daughters, and I'd missed it because I'd spent most of the morning moping around. I did not know what was happening to me but since Friday I had not been in the best of moods. Once I told Fiona I was not coming to Storm Eagle, I started looking deep within, so deep that I slipped into an ocean of pity and other negative and dark emotions that would have made a most pitiful bowl of mud salad. Did a part of me wish I could go, to meet my teachers in person, to meet Lynn, to melt into these ancient teachings which have offered a gateway to my creativity? Although I knew that right now was not the right time, that it might even be a distraction more than a growth to go, I still felt an awful despair. My life had built a fence around me, each post representing prayer, family, work, service, patience, duty. Every so often, the fence stretched wider to create more pasture for me to play in, but the stretching also caused the instillation of more posts with similar representations.

A blue jay flew in from the west and landed on my back porch. Through the window which faced my computer, I pleasantly observed his blue, white, and black plumage. I googled his totem and found that, among many things, he teaches lessons of adaptation to any situation and the importance of balancing one's power with silence and patience. Blue jays are known for their intelligence and complex social systems with tight family bonds. Their favorite food is acorn, which, according to Cornell Lab of Ornithology, is credited to them helping spread oak trees after the last glacial period.

We made it to church late, as usual. I checked the kids into their respective rooms on the second floor and then I rushed downstairs, headed to the café. Coffee in hand, I entered the room where the music pastor sang a song that brought the congregation into a holy union, their arms swaying high in the air like trees on a windy day. I took out my journal, planner, iPhone, and pen and, along with my coffee, placed them on the empty chair beside me. Then I began to take notes.

Pointing at a map on the projector, Pastor Aaron talked quite a bit about Nineveh Plains. He said, "Nineveh was like any major city in the US. Nineveh, the capital of Assyria, was the superpower of her day. It required three days to circle metropolitan Nineveh."

Nineveh was an ancient Mesopotamian city on the eastern bank of the Tigris River. It is one of the oldest and greatest cities in antiquity. The area was settled as early as 6000 BC and by 3000 BC had become an important religious center for worship of the goddess Ishtar.

"And the Ninevites lived large," he said. "They enjoyed the best chariots, the finest food, and the most exotic entertainment. It had an extensive business and commercial system like none in the world. In addition, Assyria had ruled the world for two-hundred years and was the strongest military power." He paused, looked around and asked, "Sounds familiar?"

He added that Nineveh's wickedness was great, and unbeknownst to them, their days were numbered. It would not be long before Babylon would overtake Nineveh. God gave them one last chance to repent, however, by sending Jonah. After Jonah's sermon to them, the entire city turned from their sin of violence, which they were known for, and turned to God.

Yet, in my opinion, they must have once again gone back to their old ways because, over the years, Nineveh fell into several dictatorships, including the Ottoman and Saddam's Baath Party. More recently, the Radical Islamic State of Iraq and Syria (ISIS) destroyed shrines belonging to two biblical prophets – high revered by both Christians and Muslims: Prophet Jonah, dating back to the eighth century BC, and Prophet Daniel.

Some have suggested that if America continues to turn plump and idle, if it continues to forsake the Divine, it too will one day end up with a similar fate to that of Nineveh. George Kirkpatrick wrote that America, which he describes as "ease crazed," *is* a modern day Nineveh.

"Shouldn't we be concerned with Sterling Heights, with that great city and its surrounding cities? We're kingdom minded! Wherever people go to worship makes us happy! Send me to the city of Sterling Heights and its surrounding cities. Help me plant seeds in here!"

I thought about the barrel of journals that sat quietly in the corner of my office, which I had not looked at for over ten years. "You are sitting on a treasure chest," Susan, my part-French, part-Native American teacher once said to me. Not long from now I will open that barrel and see what is inside. I have so much work ahead of me, so much wonderful work.

"God made you for an extraordinary life," Pastor Aaron said passionately, "a life that can change the world. Are you willing to change the world?"

My answer was yes, but first I had to detach from all attachments to material and monetary rewards and to live my life perfecting my art of writing. A few days later I found myself in the hospital.

Chapter 24
AN EVENTFUL DEATH

I arrived to the hospital shortly after midnight. The entrance doors locked, I had to use the buzz-in security system for visitors to be allowed inside. I took the elevator to the second floor and searched for room 210. Her lights were turned off and she laid sound asleep, wrapped in layers of white bed sheets and a blanket. A nurse came in and asked if I needed anything.

"Can I have a cup of coffee? There are no hot drinks in the vending machines."

"Sure, I'll be right back."

I relaxed in one of the chairs and watched the slow, gentle rhythm of my mother's breathing. Just a few hours earlier I had submitted the revised manuscript to the editor and the first thing on my mind was to visit my mom since I hadn't seen her in ten days. I called to see how she was doing and found out that my sister had taken her to the ER. She had fallen and fractured her back. Once my husband came home, I rushed to the hospital to be by her side.

My mom opened her eyes and looked at me with confusion. "Weam, what are you doing here?"

"I came to see you."

"Why did you come?"

"To see you."

Her expression turned innocent. "Why are there tears on

your face?"

I looked away, grabbed a Kleenex, and tried to collect myself. The nurse came in to check my mother's vital signs. My mother observed the nurse in admiration. "They have the best people here," she said to me in Arabic.

"What did she say?" the nurse asked.

"She said they have the best people here."

"Oh, that is so sweet," the nurse said, touched. "Thank you."

"I swear, Weam, your uncle's wife should come and live here," my mom said. "She'd have nothing to worry about here. It's quite nice and lovely."

She made me laugh. The nurse asked what my mom said and I interpreted. After the nurse left, my mom told me of the day's events. My sister had taken her to the doctor's. Later they returned home and she had a lunch of string bean stew with rice. After that, one of my sisters visited her.

"How long have you been at the hospital?" I asked.

"I'm not at a hospital."

"Yes, you are at a hospital," I said, taken aback.

"No, I'm not."

"This isn't a hospital?"

"No," she said.

"Then what is it?"

"It's a home."

"Whose home?"

"These three women who keep coming in and out," she said, most confidently.

I was speechless.

"Why are you crying? Did you have a fight with Sudaid?" she asked, laughing knowingly.

"No."

"Then why are you crying?"

"Sudaid got his citizenship a few weeks ago," I said, barely able to speak but wanting to change the subject.

"He did? God bless!" She looked around. "I swear the people in this house are the best. Saad's people are really good."

I laughed through my tears. My brother-in-law Saad knew a lot of hospitable people, and she thought that these women were in some way, shape, or form connected to him.

"I feel nauseous," she said. "And I'm very hungry."

I told the nurse. She said she'd bring food from the cafeteria and handed me a pink plastic container. I placed it under my mother's chin and she threw up. She said she felt better afterward.

"Good thing you came," she said to me in Arabic.

"Good thing you came," the nurse said to me in English. She'd returned with a chicken Caesar wrap and a Light & Fit peach yogurt. My mother hurriedly ate half the sandwich, looking like a baby without her dentures.

"Wow, she is hungry," said the nurse.

After she finished her sandwich, she wanted to use the bathroom, but she couldn't get up. I helped the nurse with the bedpan and noticed my mother's unusually weak muscles. Her condition saddened me but I felt happy to have this opportunity to be near her.

"What is on your mind, Mom?" I asked.

"I no longer have a mind, daughter."

She slept fairly well, except when woken up by a nurse wanting to check her vital signs. Around 7:30 am, I opened the shades and saw beneath my mom's room a roof carpeted with pebbles. It was still dark. Hundreds of birds suddenly flew above us, going north. I stared at them until their bodies became as tiny as a dot, and then I left the window. I called the cafeteria to order breakfast before leaving to go home. I had to return in time for my husband to take my daughter to school.

"What do you want to eat, Mom?" I asked, looking over the menu.

"Whatever."

"Do you want eggs or pancakes?"

"Whatever you choose."

"You're eating it, Mom, not me. What would you like?"

"Whatever they have."

I ordered French toast and coffee.

"Do you want apple or orange juice?"

"Whatever you choose."

I ordered orange juice, remembering how she liked to drink it in the morning.

At home, I went straight to bed, even though the sink had piles of dirty dishes and I still had to make lunch and clean the house. Woke up in time to cook, drop my son off at school, and attend a meeting. When I returned home, I made a small pita bread sandwich of baked eggplant and potatoes, just so I would not pass out of dizziness. Washed the dishes, made the beds, and swept before heading to the bank to make a deposit. Stopped at Krogers to grocery shop then went to the Dollar Store and Sally's to find a crown for my daughter for that night's Halloween Fest. No one had a crown.

At night, I headed to the hospital again.

The hospital staff moved my mom to the intensive care unit. Her heart was not beating at a normal pace. They might put a pacemaker in her heart, but since her age was a concern, they had to first look at other options. They would let us know tomorrow. I nodded at the doctor's words, thanked him, and sat in the chair facing my mother. I opened my journal and began to write. My mom had always timed her hospitalizations perfectly. She let me first finish my work, whether it was a college paper or a book manuscript, and then she addressed a situation that needed my full attention or her full attention or both our full attention.

I returned home in time for my scheduled phone session with Fiona. I told her about my mom's situation and how it was creating some conflict and tension between the siblings.

"Is it possible that your mother, in the hospital, is in fear? As she gets discharged, unconsciously, everything goes to normal and no one goes to see her anymore. She's causing a wedge between everybody and causes dis ease among everybody so she doesn't have to look at her fear. Nobody is looking at the source of the dis ease within you and within her."

I felt exhausted by our chaotic tribal issues. Everyone was close in kin, had many similarities, yet was so very different. We loved each other very much, seemed inseparable, but I was still angry at some of the past behavior of the women. I felt they had abandoned me when I needed them most.

"Let the stories go and follow the energy," she said. "Everybody is holding onto the stories. Until you see you're stuck in a story, you keep being stuck. You haven't found the thread that started this whole thread. Be grateful for this chaos. Within chaos comes change. Maybe Spirit is calling you back into yourself. You are leaving an old story and creating a new story. This old energy is going to try to get you to feed it. Power is testing you. Are you going to give away your power to something that doesn't serve you? If you don't feed it, it'll stop coming up."

Later we talked about the ancient teachings that were passed onto us. I asked, "How do I incorporate my kids into all of this?"

"Your kids are already catching onto that," she said. "They're watching, and we teach them their bad habits and their good habits. They see how you pick up that rock you told me about and communicate with it. When they imagine things, they enter a realm of magical environment. Let them express that. Our society damns and suppresses that."

She told me the story of how she'd collected many, many stones over time. There was a little girl who, when she was four, would knock on Fiona's door to come look at the stones.

"It's so much fun to get muddy and dirty. Instead of playing with playdough, let them build mud and let it dry." She was quiet for a few seconds, then said," What you are doing now is going to affect generations to come. What you are doing is huge. You're breaking what seven generations of people have been doing. You're creating a new story. You're giving your kids and their kids and their kids more heart than they've ever gotten. You're clearing energy for them because you're clearing energy for you. You are learning to be a good digger. You are given an opportunity to be pushed."

I listened attentively.

"I want you by Sunday to send me a question you want to ask Lynn during her next conference call and by tomorrow or Friday evening, to write the scholarship application for the school. Did you receive the application in the email I sent you last week?"

"Oh, I had forgotten about the application and had actually planned to skip it."

"Look at why you wouldn't do it. What are you protecting?"

"To be honest, I'm tired of rejections. While I have received a lot of acceptances in the past, the things that would have played a major role in my life were rejected. With the last rejection let-ter, I even cried. I'd spent so much time on the application."

"It took me two weeks to write my application. I would cry, and I couldn't do it. My father would always say, 'We don't need anything. Someone else needs it more than us.' That's not neces-sarily true. It is his feelings. So with regards to the scholarship, I felt unworthy. Then I wrote it and all the windows and doors started getting opened. It was freeing once I sent it. I didn't give a shit if I got it or not. But I did want the validation."

"Did you end up getting the scholarship?"

"Yes." We were quiet. "Just express yourself honestly and truthfully when you apply. Part of your healing is getting over your fear of rejections."

"Okay, I'll apply for the scholarship."

"And give thanks to yourself. Thank yourself to yourself constantly."

My husband and I went to Kroger and had our children pick out the pumpkins they wanted to decorate for Halloween. There was tension between us. He complained that I was the only one of my siblings spending every night at the hospital. Why weren't the others taking turns, he wondered? The few that did go did so occasionally, unlike me, who went every day. And, he added, when I was not at the hospital, I was on the phone arranging the schedule for who was going to go and stay at the hospital.

My mother did not speak English, and the hospital did not have an interpreter. We wanted someone there at all times to be able to communicate with the doctors and nurses and so my mother would not feel abandoned, yet the lack of cooperation made me want to once again divorce the siblings I had recently reconciled with.

"I don't care what everyone else does or does not do," I said to him. "This is my choice."

The truth was, I sensed my mother would die soon and I did not want her to die alone. I decided I would skip tonight to spend time with my family.

"I picked the poofect pumpkin," my son said proudly as we drove home.

I started a fire and placed a towel and the pumpkins on the fireplace bench. My children happily painted their pumpkins as I put groceries away. My husband went with my brother-in-law to visit my mom. An hour later, he returned home, his eyes sad and red. He said, "You should go and stay with your mom today."

I rushed into my room, changed, and when I got to the hospital, I saw one of my sisters-in-law sitting outside my mother's room, talking on the phone. She hung up and we kissed.

"How is she doing?" I asked.

"Not too good. She barely ate anything, and she hasn't gone to the bathroom in hours. Things are not right."

I broke down crying.

"I'm sorry," she said. "Your brother was here earlier. He too broke down crying."

I walked inside my mother's room. She was in a deep sleep. I held her hand, kissed her arms and face, and prayed. "God, I want her to stay, but I don't want her to suffer. Can You make both possible?" I repeatedly called out "Mom," but she would not respond. I forced her to wake up. I wanted her to see me. She couldn't open her eyes. I kept calling her name and she finally opened them, startled. She stared at me.

"Why are you crying?" she asked.

I couldn't speak.

"Why are you crying?"

"I'm scared for you."

"Don't be scared."

"Do you want water?"

"No."

"Do you want anything?"

"No."

"Are you hungry?"

"No."

I kissed and hugged her. She kissed me back. She looked very lethargic, her skin hard, dry, and flaky. Her tongue had a few white dots. She only moved to bring up her index finger. She would stare at the red light on the plastic clamp that was attached to her index finger. The device measured the oxygen in her blood. After staring at the red light, she would rest her finger on her forehead.

I pulled my chair closer to her bed and slept with my hands touching her feet. I felt where her feet have been, in the streets of Baghdad, going back and forth to the souk, carrying one child after another after another, twelve children in all, going up stairs to the rooftop to hang the laundry on a rope or to prepare the beds for summer. The memories of her in America then flowed in, when she would clean the entire house, cook, and wait for me to return from work, to take her to either one of my sister's homes, to the produce market, or to a doctor's appointment.

Once, when I was still single and living under her roof, I read the coffee grains in her cup. I asked her, "What do you want?"

"I want to live," she said.

I watched her breathe. On a few occasions, her heartbeats seemed to stop. The sight paralyzed me. But then I saw the motion of her breathing, and yet I felt little or no relief. I felt any second now she would die. My eyes searched for distractions: her yellow bracelet that said "Fall Risk," the flowers and chocolate on the windowsill, and the Virgin Mary statuette in a glass box decorated with sea shells. The Virgin Mary wore a deep green veil with sequins, and inside the box it said *Ruega Senora por Nosotros*, Senora, Pray for Us.

I noticed I had used up the roll of toilet paper to wipe my tears and nose and had made a big mound of it on the table. I picked up the menu and read, *Chef Connection: your personalized dinning service, call 4243 (4-Chef). Each food item has the number of carbs it contains. To control blood sugar, each meal plan should not go over four carbs.*

The time was 3:52 am. I had barely slept since I got here.

"Is your neck hurting you?" I asked after watching her rub her neck for a while.

"Yes."

"You want me to rub it?"

"It's up to you."

I rubbed it.

"You want water?" I asked.

"No."

"Food?"

"No."

"Do you want me to do anything for you, Mom?"

"No."

In the past, I had accompanied my mom to the hospital many times and she would often ask for this or that. Not today. It was as if her spirit was already gone.

The next day, I arrived just before midnight. My mother was sound asleep.

"I hope your lady is going to be okay." A woman's voice came from the other side. "Is she afraid of the dark?"

I went around the curtain that separated the beds. A large-size lady was there.

"Is your lady afraid of the dark?" she asked again.

"My mom does not know how to speak English, so my siblings and I have been switching shifts to translate for the hospital staff."

She told me her story. She was seventy-one years old, and after the hospital had a pacemaker put in three months ago, she went for a checkup and they discovered a wire out of place. "I don't know if the doctor put it in wrong to begin with or if I did something to move it," she said. "You know, they don't tell you anything. But they said it's now fixed. I'm supposed to be released tomorrow, but maybe I should stay another day. At home, I have to help my husband and if you saw us, it's like the blind leading the blind. But I have a dog, and I know he really misses me and I miss him."

"I have two kids at home."

"And a husband?"

"Yes."

"Oh, so you have three kids."

I laughed.

"Well, husbands are like kids," she said.

"Yeah, my husband was grouchier about me leaving the house than they were."

"That's why after I had one kid, I kept my legs crossed. I told him if you come near me, I will kill you."

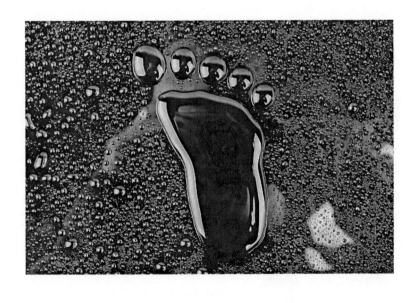

Chapter 25
JUST DIVE IN

I sat at Barnes & Noble and prepared for the next book, *The Mystery School*, while my mentors, other apprentices, and Lynn Andrews settled into the first day of Storm Eagle. I was not with them, but I was happy that I had won the scholarship, which paid part of my school tuition. I had also had my version of a spiritual quickening at the hospital next to my mom. My mother was transferred the next day to Cherrywood Nursing and Living Center for rehab. I brought hummus and soup for her to eat. Her room had a beautiful view of rolling hills, trees, and a sidewalk painted with freshly fallen autumn leaves. I pushed her wheelchair in front of the glass slide door, and we watched the strong wind raise the leaves into midair, where they drifted to and fro. She stared ahead in utter silence and blankness. My son sat on a chair, playing on his iPad. I wrote in my journal.

"May everything you touch turn into gold," my mother said to me.

"Thank you."

Sunday we went to church. The topic was regret. The pastor asked that we face the regrets of our lives and then move into the freedom that God intended us to live. We have to work through our regrets, he said. As Christians, we know that we have been forgiven but we know that we made those choices, and the regret still haunts us, as in the case of parenting. We get caught up with the pains of the past and try to be gateways to our children's own experiences.

"I notice many Christians are stuck in past regrets," Pastor Aaron said. "When you focus too long on your mistakes, it becomes your identity, it becomes your Scarlett Letter. Regrets are difficult because you can't change them. That frustrates people. That frustrates me. They are in our past but sometimes it affects those around you or your future. Regret can lead to paranoia. It can be the prison cell, and you are the warden. How many people know of someone who, no matter what you're talking about, go back to an issue that has since imprisoned them and it has emotionally paralyzed them?"

I wanted to raise my hand before reminding myself it was a rhetorical question.

"I don't believe that God intended for us to live in bondage and suffering but rather a powerful life," he said. He gave a number of verses from the bible and concluded. "Regret comes in like a flood and can easily overwhelm us. Guilt sours the flavor of freedom and makes us live with this is what I deserve. Jesus wants no part of that for you. Jesus is not okay with you living beneath his plans for you. God makes all things new! I'm emotional today because I'm tired of Christians living beneath what Jesus intended them to be. Today I encourage you to see Jesus on the shore. But we're standing on the boat saying, 'I think that's the Lord but I'm not sure. I'm not sure I can make it to the shore.' And he's saying, 'Just dive in!'"

Just dive in. I placed an exclamation point after these three words and closed my notebook.

After church, I went to my yoga class. Despite writing an article earlier in the year about how some Christians think yoga is against the Christian faith, I had happily restarted yoga practice after seeing it was part of our school curriculum. On the way home, as I entered one of our subdivision streets, I saw rows and rows of cars parked in the street.

"Why are there so many cars, Mamma?" my daughter asked.

"There must be a wedding!" I said, remembering it was a Sunday.

I looked for the house with the bride or groom and was shaken by the sight of a large group of Chaldean people dressed in black.

"Oh, it's a funeral," I said, disheartened.

"What's a funeral, Mom?" my kids asked.

"It's a ceremony that honors someone who died, like a wedding honors two people getting married."

"We went to a funeral before, remember?" my daughter said.

"No, you didn't!"

"Yes, we did. Remember Sandy's son?"

"Oh, yeah," I said, remembering the burial of my niece's newborn son.

By midnight I was back at Beaumont Hospital, where an ambulance had transferred my mother because she could not keep any food or liquid down and the nurses feared she would dehydrate. *You are being cared for by the blue team.* I read the sign on the wall as I fell asleep.

"Room eighty-two is not in her bed?" Maria, the Romanian nurse, spoke into a small wireless phone. "Check the bathroom and call me back."

I drowsily observed her excitement. The sun had come up with its orange and yellow colors. Maria returned the phone to her pocket and continued to give my mother her pills. Another nurse came in and said, "Eighty-two is not in her room."

The two quickly scurried out of the room, and I heard them talk about the missing eighty-two. Someone asked, "Should we call security?"

"Yes," Maria said.

"I prayed so hard to go home, girl," the elderly woman in the second bed said. "Jeez, I miss my bed! Sleeping on the hospital bed is like sleeping on rocks. And the nurses come in throughout the night so you can't even sleep. You know how it is if you've ever stayed in a hospital."

Fiona came back from Storm Eagle. I told her about the fear and panic that overtook me when my mother entered the hospital. On several occasions, we thought she would die. It was horrific because I felt we were not done yet. I still had so much to tell her, much love to give her. I also wanted to hear her out rather than focus on the negative aspects that had butchered our relationship. Her near-death experience shifted my perspective and caused me to want to live in the now.

"The importance of now becomes essential," Fiona said. "Maybe do a wheel with the center being the negative and a wheel with the positive in the center and have a heart-to-heart conversation with your mom. This may be a beautiful thing that may get her talking. You can involve your children, and see if they have questions for their grandma. This will bring history forward through their eyes. Their questions can be amazing and will make them know that they are worthy, that their questions are important."

"My mother and I have had many misunderstandings be-cause we are so different. I wanted to explore the world, and she didn't."

"Her world is her home," Fiona said. "That's why she could not understand or help you with your needs. She has no desire to look outside."

"My mother taught us the biggest lessons about marriage, and mostly through example."

"What did she teach?"

I tried to describe it accurately and with as few words as possible. It took a while before I said, "She knew how to stay put."

"Hmmm."

"She did it so well that even a tornado could not move her. She'd move the tornado."

Fiona laughed.

"That's what I did with my husband. I shifted his energy so that it was more aligned with my harmony. Looking back, all my sisters did that with their husbands. It's really the same with most of the women from her tribe."

I told her how grateful I was for the extra time with my mom, how I would no longer let excuses stop me from getting close to her. I noticed that in the hospital we shared more intimate time. Elsewhere, the visits consisted of multitudes of people and the conversations would steer in directions that had little to do with her. My attempts to get to know her would cave in by a large spider's web that was made up of many peoples' dramas and noise.

"You want to get to know her," she said. "Going through the school, you play many roles, and now this is your new role with your mom. You might want to use a talking stick so you cannot cut her off while she's holding it. You just have to listen. If you are not comfortable using a talking stick, hold anything that will remind you to be silent."

My parents had a big age and educational difference between them. She was only twelve years old when they got married. He was thirteen years her senior. She was a simple farm girl who'd never went to school. He was a well-educated man from a well-educated family. This must have been difficult for both of them, but with my mom probably more. I remembered her often saying, whenever we made light of her comments, "You're like your father. You don't value my words." It was difficult listening to her complain about my father, especially since he was dead and we had good memories of him. He was an open-minded, optimistic, and just man. He passed onto us a sense of confidence and a desire for knowledge.

Only now could I see how much pain and wisdom my mother had suppressed.

"It's easy to put someone deceased on a pedestal," Fiona said. "If it was your dad telling the story, would you jump in and defend your mom or would you let him tell the story?"

"Where is that prejudice from?"

"That's another thing you can put on the wheel," she said. "There's never, ever, ever going to be someone like your mom, not from now to eternity. Same with you. Same with your daughter. No one will ever, ever, ever have the same experience."

"I must let my mother talk without interrupting her or defending my dad," I said, earnestly.

"Where does the sense of having to defend someone come from? There's nothing to defend." She was quiet, and added, "You are entering into another hoop of power because you're seeing things differently."

Our time nearly up, I brought up the church I had been going to for a year, how I did not realize the type of church it was until about a month ago, when the pastor said "Pentecostal." I did not know what that word meant and looked it up online once I returned home. According to Wikipedia, Pentecostalism is a renewal movement within Protestant Christianity that places special emphasis on a direct personal experience of God through the baptism with the Holy Spirit. The term Pentecostal is derived from Pentecost, the Greek name for the Jewish Feast of Weeks. For Christians, this event commemorates the descent of the Holy Spirit upon the followers of Jesus Christ, as described in the second chapter of the *Book of Acts.*

"A few people have made negative comments about me going to a church outside of our culture," I said. "I hope that their criticism doesn't affect how I feel about it."

"It only will if you let it. If you're a beautiful model for your kids, allowing them to follow their feelings, the big teaching you're giving them is to follow their heart. Categorizing religion is what starts barriers. One year you went without even knowing what type of church it was. That's a beautiful story in itself."

It was a beautiful story, but there was more to it than that. I further studied Pentecostalism to learn how it relates to shamanism. Based on what I found, Pentecostalism is as close to shamanism as formal Christianity gets. It involves mediation with an individual that has metaphysical abilities, which are used for the good of the community that they are a part of. In "The Shamanic Complex in the Pentecostal Church," an article by Kevin Horwartt, the author writes about the similarities:

> Both shamans and Pentecostal preachers profess a connection between the spiritual world and the mundane. The power they receive through their contact allows them to act as spirits because of their privileged posi-

tion. More important, the events that take place in both ritual systems take place a in a spiritual context.... In both cultures, those in need of cure are in some way customarily denied the freedom of expression, or impact on their surroundings, that is crucial for mental health; the healing ritual is most effective in curing illnesses that arises from psychosocial stress and the ceremony is also beneficial to those who participate because they also enter an ecstatic state and their mythos is stabilized well. Thus, I am convinced that the two traditions serve the same function.

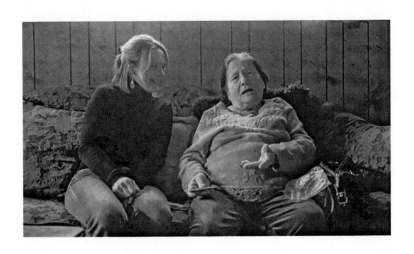

Chapter 26
THE FRENCH FILMMAKERS

I dreamt that I went into a room with a lot of people but all I could see was my daughter. I rushed and knelt in front of her, hugging her tight and really missing her. I had left her with some people for evidently a long while. They were nice, but not family, and the place was like a classroom setting. When I tried to stand up, I couldn't. My body ached, and I was stuck in a kneeling position. I thought, "Oh, from the days of sleeping in the hospital next to my mom." I finally got up and prepared to leave with her.

Brushing the dream aside, I got out of bed, made myself a cup of coffee, and prepared to interview Claire Jeantet and Fabrice Caterini through Skype, two French filmmakers I met in spring, when they came from France to the United States to film a web documentary series called *My Beloved Enemy: Iraqi American Stories*. They had contacted me through a friend because they wanted to interview Warina Zaya Bashou, who, at 111 years old, became the second oldest person to be granted a US citizenship. They wanted to cover an interesting story about an elderly Iraqi attaining their citizenship and hoped I could introduce them to Warnia since I had previously written an article about her. Warina lived only a few blocks from my house, but when I called her family, they told me she had passed away.

I told them to come over and perhaps I could help them

find another subject. An hour later three beautiful and gracious French people came to my door – Claire, an attractive blonde woman, and two tall and dark handsome men, Fabrice and Thomas Bernardi, the chief cameraman. We had a little brunch, and they ended up interviewing my mom, who was visiting, about her experience in attaining her citizenship in 1997. At that time, I had helped her memorize fifty questions and answers about the United States, in Arabic, and I was permitted to be her interpreter during examination. She had to get seven out of ten questions right. She only got one wrong answer.

"Why did you want to get your citizenship?" Claire, the director, asked her.

"I wanted to be like my children," my mother said, and I interpreted. "They all got their citizenship, and so it was now my turn."

I told the filmmakers how the day of her naturalization I was in a hurry to go to work. My mother wanted to take a picture with the judge, like other people had lined up to do. I did not see the point in a picture. I had not taken one when I received my citizenship. We left and ever since, when I thought about that day, I wished I had reacted differently. I did not realize it then, but this was the first major accomplishment for her outside of her home. She was proud to have received a document that honored her efforts, a reward, something that validated she had capabilities other than being a good housewife and mother.

"Now she got more than that picture that she had wanted sixteen years ago," I said.

We laughed.

In September, the filmmakers showed the documentary at Visa pour L'Image, the premiere International Festival held in Perpignan, France.

"Oh Weam, your mother up there on the screen made a real impact," Claire told me through Skype. "The audience loved her."

Her words further illuminated what I had already begun to understand about my mother. This woman, born in a village and never having gone to school, although she wished she had, impacted not only her children's lives, but her story had landed in France and later traveled the world through the internet. And at eighty-years-old, she was not done yet. Yes, I inherited my love for words and books, and my desire to heal, from my father, but I could not have made my dreams come true without my mother's teachings of discipline and faith in a higher power.

"How is your book coming along?" Claire asked.

"I'm going through a final critique, *hopefully*, and I've already begun my next project, which deals with ancient teachings, mostly those which pertain to the feminine power. With a memoir, I look at women and the dynamics between her and her relationship with the modern day world. One of the relationships I examine is the mother/daughter relationship, in my case, as it is lived by a tribal culture."

"This sounds like a very fascinating subject," she said.

"The only problem is getting my mom to talk."

Once our Skype call ended, I got my daughter ready for school, and after I dropped her off, went to visit my mother at Heartland Rehab where she had been transferred from the hospital the night before. It was a cold November morning with light snow. When I walked into her room, she sat in bed, the breakfast tray in front of her. She stared out into space, her food untouched.

"What's wrong, Mom?"

"I don't feel good."

"Why?"

"I don't know."

"Why aren't you eating?"

She didn't answer. I began adding butter and syrup to her French toast, then cut it into small pieces. She ate with a dead heart. I told her what the French filmmakers said, that her film was shown on a movie screen and the audience loved her.

Her eyes brightened. "Really?"

I pulled my chair closer to her bed. "Mom, before you got married, did your parents ask for your opinion or did they just marry you off?"

"They asked for my opinion."

"And you approved?"

"Yes."

"What did they say to you?"

She waved her hand. "Don't give me a headache. I already have one."

I laughed. "Why do you have a headache?"

"I don't know. I just do."

"Which church did you get married in?"

"The one by our house."

"In Telkaif or Baghdad?"

"Baghdad."

"Did you wear a wedding dress?"

She laughed. "Yes, of course."

"Who bought your dress?"

"I didn't wear a wedding dress."

"You didn't? Why?"

"Your dad couldn't afford it."

"What did you wear?"

"A gown."

"Who bought it?"

"He did."

"Did you have a party?"

"There was a gathering at his father's house in Baghdad."

The nurse came in and gave her some medications. My mother vomited after swallowing the large pill for potassium, and then she quickly fell asleep. I wrote in my journal as I watched the show *Kelly and Michael*. Before I left, I stared at her for a few moments as she slept soundly in peace and contentment. The scent of death was very, very near, and like she always said, no one knew when it would summon her to the other world.

I left the rehab absorbed in sadness and guilt. Her condition dragged out emotions that had been neatly tucked away, forgotten, and I had to deal with them like dusty articles, asking myself, should I keep them or get rid of them? I placed the piles of emotions on the Sacred Wheel to examine them more carefully, and the confusion was reduced to one truth: We had failed her. She did not say that, not in speech, but in her expressionless face as she abandoned herself to a dark misery.

I spent the rest of the week focusing on school assignments and doing housework. I listened to Lynn's CDs way into the night, as late as 3 am as I folded clothes, sorted mail, and paid bills. My mom improved a little over time. One day I was able to get her to take five walking steps. She had kept saying "I can't," but I insisted that she could and finally I firmly said to her, "Don't talk! Focus!" After she took the steps, she was impressed with herself. It validated for her that she could and will walk again.

Over the phone, Fiona told me she was sitting near a fireplace, like me. She'd just finished chopping wood earlier and figured, why not just enjoy it?

"Isn't it warm where you are?" I asked.

"It's about forty degrees."

I imagined her relationship with the outdoors, the axe in her hand thrusting through wood, releasing negative emotions and creating a society with nature; the air of the winter season whispering all sorts of wisdom in her lungs; the splitting and the stacking of the wood that she would later transport to a fire pit, where the wood would continue to give of itself for others' enjoyment.

"So, what has been going on with you?" she asked.

"I've been spending time alone, just reflecting and preparing for something new. I just don't know what it is yet. I feel like I'm window shopping."

"Continue to window shop, but don't make any big purchases yet," she said. "It's like right now you're getting ready to write a new story and deciding what the plot will be."

"I want to change some of the people in my life," I said.

"No, it has nothing to do with the other person. The only thing you are responsible for is yourself. What can you do to honor the part of you that is wanting to change? People will change if you change. You are part of the pattern that keeps recurring. If you want to change, you have to first change the pattern."

"How do I do that?"

"Go into silence, go to the part that is calling for you and get to know it and see what it's trying to say to you, and ask it, how do you want to be honored? It wants to be heard and that part of you has started to hear it."

I complained that in the past ten days, several situations

occurred that held up mirrors for me. People would take advantage of and disrespect my time and then return with a smile, like nothing had happened. I would respond kindly when actually I wanted to be genuine and tell them, "This is not right. You are rude and inconsiderate for cancelling on me this and that many times, etc. I'm tired of playing these games."

"Aren't you playing a game now?" Fiona asked. "Isn't what you're doing playing a game?"

It was. By having the attitude that all was A-okay, I was playing.

"Ask yourself what can make you genuine? Create a scenario with yourself, if I had to do it all over again, if my genuine self would have to do it all over again, how would you want me to respond? Write it out, but don't send it. You can print and burn it to release the energy, and keep a copy for yourself in order to hold onto the genuine part that you want to come out. That way, by not sending it, you are not upsetting the other person. Until you want it to be published – your genuine self, that is – and show it to the world."

"I feel the genuine self is already coming out."

"You're strengthening the muscle."

I went on to tell her about a relative's constant critical behavior toward me.

"When are people most critical?" she asked.

"When they are insecure."

"Who is she not looking at?"

"Herself," I said, remembering what my previous Native American teachers had taught me. "Luckily, I don't fall for people's criticism like before. Nor does it upset me like before."

"You've dropped the rope in the tug of war."

My daughter asked if she could make hot cocoa and after I

said yes, she rushed to get out of the cupboard the vintage *How to Make an American Quilt* movie mugs, a promotional item that Universal Studies gave our family-owned video store in the mid-1990s.

"That woman is the mirror, but it's your pattern that has to change," she said. "You're circulating yourself."

In past relationships, when the person, male or female, wanted to end the relationship, I assumed it was somehow my fault and tried to fix the situation by showing more compassion and kindness. Playing the role of a saint, I excused and forgave their crude behavior and naturally, they continued to throw emotional blows at me. My insecurities prevented me from seeing the truth and letting go. It wasn't until I met Chip and Susan that I began to understand the importance of honoring my own feelings, not just those of others. They'd said to me, "In any relationship, if you are only giving or only receiving, then there is an imbalance. That's when the essence of the relationship is no longer about love but about control."

"I thought those stories were over with," I told Fiona.

"You're over the people in those stories, but it's a pattern you have to change," she said. "It's a cellular memory response you're doing. You're tired of getting burned, and you have to find ways to not get burned. You can, for instance, not get burned by the following methods: turn the stove off, use a pot holder, do not put the stove too high."

My daughter carefully returned with her mug in the palm of her hands, my son following her with his mug. A few drops of hot cocoa failed to stay within the perimeter of the mug, dropping to the floor. As they placed their mugs on the fireplace bench, I watched the tiny marshmallows floating on top quickly dissolve into the hot cocoa.

"Once a teacher shared an experience she had during her shamanic practice," Fiona said after a long silence. "There was a circle of about ten to twelve people. Each one took a turn standing in the center and everyone else would throw insults at that person. She stood there in the center, taking the insults thrown at her until she realized she did not have to stand in the center. She could just leave the center."

The Red Indian once told me, "If there's fighting and killing on a land, move, go elsewhere. You don't have to fight back."

"Once you know who you are, you will not need validation," Fiona said.

Chapter 27
SEEING MY HANDS IN MY DREAM

My husband left for Jordan the day before my birthday. He wanted to visit his parents whom he had not seen in thirteen years. My brother dropped him off at the airport that morning.

"This is going to be a new day, right, Mamma?" my son asked in the car as I drove him to preschool.

"Yes, it is," I said, watching him through the rear view mirror.

The rest of the day was mellow. After school my daughter took a very long nap. That night we sat around the fireplace as I cleaned out my office, tossing unwanted papers into the fire and filing the rest. The kids did their homework. I wanted to use the two weeks that my husband was away to iron our home, to smooth out any energetic wrinkles that were too subtle to detect when the home was inhabited by a good deal of activity.

The next day, my birthday, I was scheduled to speak to Fiona at night. It was a new moon, and again my children and I gathered around the fireplace. I intensely watched the flames, allowing my soul to enter their depth and tread to a faraway valley, to a time when my ancestors dreamed me here. Was I born of a collective consciousness that flirted throughout the ages with various feminine physical languages and now wanted to feel the tradition and roles of this kingdom? A day will come when my spirit will rise high again, free itself from limitations or boundaries, and join my ancestors' collective consciousness to create a new dream.

I called Fiona and said, "This is the last conversation for this year, and there is one thing I want to address before I go into the third year. I've come to terms with much of the issues between myself and my family, friends, work colleagues, and of course my husband and children. But with regards to my in-laws, there's a wedge between us that I want to remove."

"Why now?" she asked.

"One day I met an Asian spiritual man who invited me to his home for sushi. I went with my sister and daughter and we met his wife and children. I told him about my struggles in my work. In response, he recounted this story: a barren woman wanted to get pregnant, so she went to a guru for help. The guru asked her, 'Are your in-laws good people?' She said, 'Yes.' So he said, 'Then you should be good to them too.' The barren woman left the guru, changed her relationship with her in-laws, and then she became pregnant."

Since the Asian man shared this story with me, each time I heard of a woman who was not kind to her in-laws, I didn't like it. I wondered if I had been too hard on my in-laws, half of whom were in the US and the other half, including the parents, was in Jordan. Although we were quite civil toward each other, we had encountered some cultural misunderstandings and I had saved a few drops of grudges against them. I kept a distance in order to protect my space.

"I'm not sure it was necessary to do all that," I told Fiona. "I'm afraid that somehow my attitude is contributing to my in-laws' delay in getting a visa to come to the US."

My father-in-law had sworn he would never leave Iraq. He

loved his home and the people of his town. He was one of the few Christians there, but he was highly respected and esteemed by his Muslim neighbors, so much so that they honored him with the title of sheik. Then in October 2010, Al Qaeda members attacked a church in Baghdad, killing 58 and wounding 78 in a bloodbath. A great number of Christian Iraqis who had sworn to stay put in Iraq packed up and left, my in-laws included. They applied for the UN program for Iraqi refugees. In it, people went through various interview phases until they received an approval or rejection for the US. My in-laws were approved two years ago, and since then they had been waiting for a visa. Each time they went to the UN office to inquire about their status, they were told, "It's undergoing security clearance." I thought, "Two years to do security clearance on a Christian man who was over eighty years old and his wife, who was almost seventy?"

"Although I do not believe that my attitude was the major contributor of my in-laws' stagnant status," I said, "I want to cleanse myself of any negative emotions or vibrations I might have against them and send them love and light so that their dream materializes and my husband can enjoy the company of his parents here in the US and my children can finally meet their grandparents."

"What are you afraid of?" Fiona asked.

"I'm afraid what it will be like once they're here, afraid of having to once again explain myself or defend my lifestyle. I have spent much of my time trying to do that with my own family and others around me. I don't want to repeat the same process I underwent before, yet I want to make peace with them. They come to mind often."

"I want you to close your eyes," she said. "Tell me where you see this fear in you."

I was silent, searching. "It's in my head."

"What do you see in your head?"

"A lot of lips."

"What are these lips doing?"

"Talking."

"Do you know who they belong to?"

"My in-laws, who are also my relatives."

"Ask these lips what they want."

I did. They answered. "They just want to get to know me."

"Talk to them. What do you want to tell them?"

"What do you want to know about me?" They answered, "Why do you isolate yourself so?" I answered, "Because I am happy here. I feel at home alone, and I'm not comfortable socializing." They said, "How can we get closer to you if you are this isolated?"

I paused.

"What do you want to say to them?" asked Fiona.

"I don't have an answer."

"Ask the lips if they can help you figure out a solution."

I did. They answered, "It would be nice if you can include us in your life."

I said, "I want you in my life too. I don't feel comfortable being far away from you, but I'm afraid of not being able to communicate my needs, wants, and limitations. I want to open the door between us, but I can only open it so much because again, I love my solitude. I worked hard to get it, and the only reason I keep a distance is so that I can protect it."

"What are the lips doing now?" Fiona asked.

"They are smiling," I said.

"Is there anything else you want to tell them?"

"From now on I'll go easier on myself and on you."

"Is there a commitment you want to make with them?"

"When I think about you from now on, I will act upon it in a loving way."

"How are they responding now?"

"It's like I melted their heart. They want to hug me."

"Ask them if they are willing to have another conversation with you before the start of your commitment."

"They are."

"Do you want to set a date for that conversation now?"

"Yes, tomorrow."

The next day, I burned incense, started a fire, and prepared to have a talk with my in-laws. I said to them, "I don't want to hold on to the past. It no longer serves me. Let's start anew."

They responded,

"Dear Weam,

We know that we have failed your expectations, but you have no idea how difficult life was for us during the wars, the life outside of Iraq, starting from scratch here in the United States, living in fear and confusion and insecurity. To us you were a foreigner. We did not feel comfortable around you because you are so Americanized in comparison to us. We did what we did based on what we knew at that time. We did not know any better, and we realized that our ways upset you. But with you, when someone disappoints you, you do not easily forgive. Plus, you let that person feel your wrath, and it becomes more difficult to break through the wall you put up. Since then we have been waiting for the situation to change. Until you opened up the conversation now, you clearly were not ready. Are you ready now?"

"Yes, I am ready. I love my husband, and I want to honor his family by including them in our life. You are good people. You are my people. I want to get to know you better too."

For a while, I remained seated next to the fireplace, staring at the reddish logs scorching in heat. The gentle smoke and circulating incense seduced me into its love garden, where there were no barriers between me and anyone else.

* * *

The Asian man I visited had also told me of another story. A man who wanted to make money was advised by a guru to clean toilets, to clean the toilets diligently and with a grateful heart. The man went home and scrubbed the surface of the toilets as if he were scrubbing a diamond ring, using a toothbrush's bristles to get into the nooks and crannies. Money started flowing in from places he would not have imagined.

I understood from this story that it is in treating tasks which may seem lowly in a sacred manner that one becomes humbled in ego while heightened in spirit. I, myself, had no qualms about cleaning toilets. My fatigue and frustration stemmed from the number of tasks I had to do. Yet while my husband was away and the snow-filled weather forced me and my children to remain indoors, what with several school closings, I decided to use my time wisely. Lynn had written the following, "Once again, we move into the season of winter, Mother Earth's gift to us of hibernation, of dreaming and being within ourselves as we allow our dreams to germinate and gain clarity before we plant them in the coming spring."

I wrote, rested, organized the entire basement, and found creative, new ways to play with my kids, including out in the snow. For unusual fun, I packed us up to spend a day at my cousin's house. After she served dinner, the children went in the bedrooms to play, her husband went to bed, and she and I cuddled on the couch with a blanket to tell stories. She told me how one day, when she was a little girl, her brother-in-law came up to her and said, "Here are four dirhams for you."

My cousin couldn't believe it. No one had given her this much money before. She held the dirhams in her hand, happily admiring them, when the same brother-in-law came up to her and said, "Can I please have two dirhams to buy the kids ice cream?"

"Sure," she said and gave him two dirhams.

A little later he came up to her and said, "Can I have a dirham to buy cigarettes?"

She gave him another dirham. A little later he came back and said, "I need to buy something. Can I please have a dirham?"

Just as easily as they had come, the four dirhams were gone.

My cousin then told me about her family's house situation, about how they'd had to move many times, more than the rest of their friends and relatives. One time she asked her dad, "Why are we always renting? Why don't we own a home?"

"Because I'm not sure yet where we should settle," he told her.

The truth was that, like my father, my uncle had mismanaged his money. He did it through gambling. This created a lot of struggle for his wife, especially after he passed away and debt collectors came knocking on his door, wanting to collect their money. "What money?" his wife asked them. "He left us with none."

My cousin and I stayed up and talked for hours, and early the next morning, her husband peeked his head into my room as I was changing my son and asked, "Weam, would you like a cup of coffee?"

"That sounds good," I said, knowing he was excited to chit-chat with me. I felt the same about chitchatting with him. He had a very rich and passionate way of telling stories. He used vivid language, placing great focus on each word, as if storytelling were a sport.

I entered the living room, where he and a large cup of coffee awaited me. The sport of storytelling was on, and he began to recount his childhood days, where he'd experienced enormous wounds that remain with him today. His parents separated early on, his father at one point kidnapping him and going off to live in another country in the Middle East. He grew up without a mom and separate from his siblings. When his father worked for long hours or far away, he sent him to a convent, where he had his share of beatings. At home, he would be watching *Smurfs* and his father would tell him to turn off the TV and learn how to cook. He told him, "I want you to learn everything so you learn how to be a survivor, so when you're alone you know skills."

He eventually came to America and reunited with his mother during his teenage years, but not long afterward, he saw that she cared only about her daughter, not the rest of her children, all boys. He said, "My mom is always like, 'I don't want to get in the mix. I don't want to get in the mix.' But where it concerns my sister, she's the first to show up with two guns in her hands."

In the background, the five caged pet cockatiels squawked loudly and the McCaw kept yelling, "Hello!"

"If my mom saw me lying on the ground and my sister kicking me and kicking me, and I'm screaming, 'Help, Mom! Help me!' She'd say, 'Oh, no, son. She's only tripping over you.'"

He demonstrated every verb he'd used, and then he stopped to yell at the kids for making too much noise. He continued with another example, again with theatrical demonstrations. "If she walked in and saw my sister holding a knife in her left hand and a heart in her right hand and she saw me on the floor, my chest cut open, my mom would say, 'Oh, look what a great sister she is! He is wounded and she's saving his heart!'"

"I was missing all the elements that make a person human, family and love," he said. "I turned out okay because I have an angel up there. It helps that I have a wife who understands me. If I didn't I would have been a whore in the street. She always pulls me to a positive zone. If she wasn't like this, I wouldn't be here talking. Women can change him, make him, break him. A woman can take a man up and flies as high as an eagle, or she can take him six feet under."

The birds squawked louder. The McCaw continued to say, "Hello!"

"Family is like a kingdom," he said. "The kingdom is as strong as the queen. King protects and provides. Queen has a bigger part for providing within, keeping the family together. My wife always pulls me to a positive zone. If she wasn't like this, my life could have turned to the worse – one, drugs; and two, alcohol. I give myself a lot of credit. I practice what I preach. I've been at the bottom and I made it."

The birds squawked louder and louder. The McCaw continued to say, "Hello!"

"Honey, can you smack the birds?" he asked his wife, and then continued. "She doesn't know how lucky she is to have a man who knows how to express himself. So anyway, nobody believed that I would give up the bachelor lifestyle because to me it was like having a cup of coffee every day. God does not make the path for you. Everything is written in the wall. My mother-in-law puts God into everything. God. God. God. If that's the case, then why was I with whores popping pills? I didn't choose to be a big time bachelor. She says just go to church and pray, and I said, 'I can't!' I have hormones. How can I pray to God when the girl in front of me is wearing a G-string and has Victoria's Secret and she's basically saying come fuck me? They're very sexual in there, and with these kinds of interruptions you can't pray."

As I listened, I noticed an emotional intelligence I did not have before. I had acquired the type of listening that my mentors gave me. I listened with my heart, like the sun absorbing energy. The lost art of storytelling had been replaced by a jitter of noisy words. When I had told Fiona I wanted to create a safe and healthy environment for my family to tell their stories, she had said, "By you making yourself available and having fun, you will create the perfect opportunity to tell stories because that's a beautiful thing, not judging or jumping or saying, 'Why would you feel that?' You have no right to say something because you haven't lived your brothers' and sisters' stories and they haven't lived yours. No one's perspective is the same. So sit with it, ask the Sisterhood when is the right time and when it's beneficial for both of you."

She had suggested I use talking sticks. Talking sticks were passed among members of a tribal council, and only the member holding the stick was free to express himself.

"It holds the power, and the person who holds the stick is the only one who can talk," she said. "No one else can interrupt. It's also a beautiful way to have conversations around the table. Make your stick and the kids can make a stick for themselves. You can actually do that with all your tools – involve the kids."

With my cousin's husband, however, I suspected that with or without a talking stick, I would not get a turn.

I could not get a hold of my husband and got worried. I knew he had visited the Holy Land for a brief trip but then he was to return to Amman. After a few days, he finally answered his phone. "The electricity was out," he explained. "The whole city was shut down because of the White Guest."

"What White Guest?"

He laughed. "Snow. Here they call it the White Guest."

I had no idea that the Middle East, accustomed to oppressive heat, was experiencing a snow storm that most locations had not seen in over a hundred years. The roads were blocked, residents were confined to their homes, and when King Abdullah II toured the capital to check on the progress of snow-removal efforts, he ended up pulling up his sleeves and helping other men push a car stuck in the snow.

After learning about the storm, my heart sank at the thought of the millions of displaced Syrians living in makeshift shelters, many of their children enduring the cold with as little as T-shirts and sandals for protection. I prayed that my husband made it home safely and I quietly went about writing the book, cleaning the house, shoveling the snow, and missing him terribly, even missing his complaints, as when he entered the house and the aroma of cumin and other strong spices assaulted his nose on the days that I experimented with ethnic dishes like Indian and Chinese. He'd behave as if he was going to gag as I quickly opened the windows and glass door. On a few occasions I used air freshener, only to realize that such a combination made matters worse.

That Sunday I went to church. The topic was *Guiding our*

Steps. The pastor said that the average attendance in January and February jumped by 28 percent. The biggest factor was New Year, when people begin to reflect on their lives as the holidays near.

"I'm going to start to go to church," he said. "But how many know that by March many people fall off from that resolution? Part of the reason that the resolution does not change is that we try to change behaviors without changing character. We have to change the inner behavior before we change the outer." He talked about ten principles to follow in order to do that, and in the end, he said, "Many people settle for good enough, but God has an awesome plan for us, and I want to utilize that not for myself, but in order to better serve Him. Let's not make resolutions this year. Let's change who we are. Let's make the coming year be a powerful change at the core of who we are."

Yes, let's, I said in my head, digesting the power of what he said. Centering myself, I decided to finish the manuscript by January 1 and to accomplish my dreams and goals no matter what I had to go through.

After the sermon, we bought a few snacks from the café before leaving church.

"Mamma, do you know how to make Dr. Pepper?" my son asked in the car.

"How?"

"There's this guy, his name is Dr. Pepper. He cut a piece of his hair and put it in the bottle of cola and he called it Dr. Pepper."

"Who told you that?"

"Cucku. She looked it up on the internet."

"Really?"

"Yeah, Mom. Seriously."

"How do you know what she says is true?"

"Because it's for real," he said. "Do you know how macaroni and cheese was made?"

"How?"

"There was this little girl. She cut a piece of her hair and her nails, mixed them together, and made the macaroni and cheese."

"Did Cucku tell you that too?"

"Yeah. She read it online."

That night I had a dream that my children and I had entered a large arena separated into many rooms. An Obama program held an event where people could pick up as many gold coins and diamond trinkets as they could find, which were laid all over the ground and on tables, then turn them in for money, similar to the process in casinos. Each piece equated to $100,000, and my children and I gathered so many, while others were busy eating their dinner and chatting, that it must have come to a couple of millions, at least. Oprah was involved in this program, even though at the start of the dream she'd criticized an issue the president was involved in.

A whole day passed before I realized this was the dream where my hands had finally appeared. They were making a fortune, and they were making this fortune not only with the support of family, but also with the support of an American president.

Chapter 28

THE END

I drove through a snow-filled road to my writer's group Christmas potluck after a long time of secluding myself from the world, allowing myself to enter a spell of reflection and grateful silence. Early in the year my goal was to surrender myself entirely to a higher power so that I did not feel a peculiar split between what I felt and what I experienced, between what I said and what I thought. As shamanism led me through a healing path, I followed intently, as though submitting to a kiss that had awakened me from a long sleep of boredom and confusion.

It took a while to find Nancy's home, but finally I found it nestled on a slope in the whiteness of the snow. I parked behind numerous cars and entered the house quite late. Everyone was already seated at the long dining table, enjoying their dinner while chitchatting. I removed my coat and wet boots, joined them, and immediately drew near their lively, even mischievous, conversations. I had missed this warm and creative heat which used to bathe my writing soul, but I had distanced myself from the heat in order to heal, grow, and write.

Once we completed our dinner, we moved to the country-style family room, where we continued lively discussions of various subjects while drinking coffee and eating sweets, until the group's leader, Mary, asked, "Did anyone bring anything to read?"

Several people, including myself, raised our hands, and Mary asked, "Weam, what did you bring?"

"The first chapter of a memoir," I said. "It's about a school I'm in right now called The Mystery School. From the start of the school, we were asked to keep a journal. That's when I knew this would be my next book, that I would write a four-part memoir series, one for each year, about my experience. I knew this because I had stopped journaling for a long time, and once the school material arrived and I started my assignments, I began to write without much labor. The words flowed like water from an open faucet. Before that, my throat felt like a clogged drain in desperate need of repair and clearing."

They listened, intrigued, as I described how the school's ancient teachings had influenced my life so far. What once resembled a bleak and monotonous routine had turned as sweet as raspberry syrup. Throughout the day I tasted spoonfuls of meaning and significance even when the spoon seemed empty. I read the first chapter and then stopped and looked up at the enormous silence. No one said a word, and then someone asked, "What kind of school is this?"

"What does it teach?" another person asked.

"Is it spiritual?" someone asked.

Soon the group of about eight people bonded together in a conversation on whether this school could possibly be of benefit to someone like me. They reached far down into the water to grab a lost oar or a fish or anything tangible to make sense of the situation. I sipped my coffee and observed them for some time before I became impatient, bounced into the water, and said, "What about the writing? What did you guys think of that?"

They liked the writing, most definitely, but they wanted to know more about the school. Amongst themselves, they began to measure its pros and cons and whether my decision to go suited my needs. Could a shamanic school actually salvage an author's literary voice? If yes, how so? Perhaps by having the lesser voices inside one's head step aside so confidence could exist? Perhaps by killing the ego or stomping on the attitude of righteousness so creativity could color the pages of the manuscript? But couldn't an author, instead, straighten out their literary spine by exercising their own will? Do they need a teacher? Did Weam do the right thing by signing up to this school?

"I'm not looking for approval about the school," I said, amused by the direction the conversation had gone to. "I just want feedback on the chapter."

"Oh, yeah, yeah. The chapter was good."

"You got me," said Elisabeth, a woman who I'd befriended years ago at the writers' group. She was once the editor-in-chief of the *Gazette van Detroit*, a Belgium newspaper, and had given me some freelance assignments. "I want to read more, to go through the journey with you. This book would also help people. It's like a service. It's intriguing. You are a stable and well-rounded person and going into it because of your writing, so it's not like you're a fairy person all into spirituality and that's it. You have a family, and you just want for your work to move forward."

"I can't believe you paid money for this school!" one Polish man said, bewildered. "I can't understand it. If you pay me a monthly fee, I could mentor you instead."

"I appreciate your offer, but no thank you," I said. "What are your thoughts about the chapter?"

"I found interesting moments to write a good short story from your childhood. If you are willing to pay me $300 a month, we can discuss this possibility."

I burst into laughter and a few other writing fellows joined me.

"Quit this Mystery School ASAP," he said, so hypnotized and disgusted at the idea of paying for a school that he could not recognize his comments were received with much merriment. "Sending energy by phone? That does not make you a writer."

One of the women, Ginny, said that she was familiar with Lynn's work. A friend had enrolled in the school and shared the teachings with her. Elisabeth, Mary, and Nancy continued to give me constructive feedback while the men analyzed the theory of the school. By the time we left Nancy's house, I realized I had another book in my hand.

The following morning, the Polish man sent me an email further expressing his disapproval of the school. He offered to give me, for $300, advice and direction, adding, "Next week I will be busy Wednesday, Tuesday, and Friday around 2 to 3 pm for physical therapy of my arm."

I told him I had to decline his generous offer and explained that currently I had to focus on and complete *The Great American Family.*

He wrote, "Good luck, I hope editing is free! Because I am afraid about scams! You will pay for editing, and no publisher! Or publisher will tell you that you will pay for printing, and you cannot sell your book without big money to promote the book! Be carefully! Check editor and agent reputation. Mostly agent are not doing editing, they only read book, and contact publishers. I did not offer you editing, because I am not English man, I am from Poland. Anyway, best wishes. And get rid of Mystery School. It is definitely a scam!"

I had a good laugh at his unconquerable belief that this school was a scam. Soon after, the editor returned my manuscript and, as I read her critique, I realized there was much more work ahead of me. But I was determined to finish the revisions before January 1. I prayed to God that He remove whatever blocks were in my way so that I could write the story with the same power, vigor, honesty, humor and freshness that is displayed in Chapter 1, which is a powerful chapter. I said, ahead of time, thank You, God, for writing the second half of the book in a clear, concise, and literary fashion. I gave Him credit for everything because all the glory and spotlight belongs to Him.

On Christmas day, my son had a fever. I took him to the after-hours clinic. The next day, I came down with the flu. I could not get out of bed and had incredible pain. The moment I lifted my head off the pillow, it throbbed like nothing I could remember having experienced before. The day after, I was in a little better shape and nearly crawled to the computer. Desperate to finish the manuscript before January 1, I shattered and destroyed the walls between me and the story and, prayer sustaining me, I got out of my head and wrote my heart out. Several days later, on the morning of December 30, I submitted the manuscript to my agent. I remained perfectly still for a few moments as the feeling of relief nestled inside of me. Then triumph tiptoed into my territory and hovered over me like the mist of a perfume. I did it! I finished the book – for now. Who knew what my agent would say about it tomorrow, how many more revisions I had to endure? But it didn't matter. For now, I would submit to the joys of baking with my children. My in-laws were coming over for New Year's Eve, as tradition had it, and I wanted to have fun in the kitchen as I prepared for the occasion.

My children suggested I check out Ro on *Nerdy Nummies* for cool baking recipes. We decided to make a Lego cake and a cream caramel. The next day, we spread food coloring dyes, eggs, condensed milk, cake batter, and other items over the kitchen counter top. Each person was assigned a task, and as I placed a hot tray of water into the oven for the cream caramel, my agent called.

"I read the manuscript," she said, breathless. She was on the treadmill.

Oh Christ, I thought. I needed a break, at least for one or two days. Once she told me about what I had to do, I would think about the work ahead of me. My desire to enjoy baking with my children was as good as dead. Dear God, when was I going to finish this book?

"That fast?" I asked.

"I worked for Jeff Kleinman. I had to read that fast."

"So what did you think?" I asked, afraid of the answer, although I figured I should get used to this by now.

"I'm going to send it to publishers as it is," she said. "You don't need to change anything."

I was shocked.

"This is scary stuff, and the story is intriguing and you can tell you've done a lot of work on it. It's totally different than the first version. I was only going to skim through it while waiting for Tim to get to the airport but once I picked it up, I couldn't put it down."

"This is what I wanted," I said. "I told the editor that I want the book to be perfect for you, and I did it."

"You did it." She laughed. "This is going to be your year, Weam."

"It's going to be *our* year!" I said, and once we hung up, I dashed into the living room, dancing the happy dance, and shouted, "I did it! I did it! I finished the book!"

My husband and children stared at me in awe. I felt new

and free.

"You're crazy," my husband said, watching me with an amusing smile.

"Yes, I am!"

I felt such bliss that I couldn't sleep. Soon I noticed that the house was unusually quiet and found that the kids had fallen asleep with their dad on our bed. After observing them for a long, long time, I went into the living room. I turned off all the lights so that only the shining Christmas lights frosted the air, and I snuggled on the couch. The essence of my daughter, when she was a newborn, drifted into my consciousness and melted my heart. Then the essence of my son, as a newborn, appeared. I felt the warmth of the sun, as if the earth decided to quickly spin to the far side to retrieve its heat waves.

I remembered Pastor Aaron's words not long ago. "Fear can be contagious," he had said. "It can be passed from generation to generation. If you grew up in a family that worries about everything, this type of fear and worry will seek the soul of a child and can affect generations until someone stands up and ends the cycle. Don't let fear come in and rob your life and your family's life."

I wrote "The End" on the story of the house that was a thousand dinars short of completion, on the three homes we lost on Pond View Drive, on the stolen inheritance land, on my married sister's disease that took her life and left her children orphans. This pattern of sabotaging our joy was going to end here, I concluded, and I fell asleep imagining what magical story awaited me in the third school year, called *Lodge of the Marriage Basket,* where we would marry the male and female aspects of ourselves.

The End

About the Author

Living in the twenty-first century, many people feel stressed and overwhelmed by life's complexities. They want to find their purpose in life. For over 25 years, I have traveled extensively and worked with wise and diverse masters who passed on teachings I would love to pass on to you through one-on-one sessions, workshops, and speaking engagements.

If you would like to learn more about how to add meaning to your life by applying this ancient wisdom, please visit my website: www.weamnamou.com or email me at Weam@WeamNamou.com

OTHER BOOKS BY HERMIZ PUBLISHING, INC.

The Feminine Art
(ISBN-13: 978-0975295625)
A novel about a married woman who distracts herself from boredom by trying to find her nephew a wife

The Mismatched Braid
(ISBN-13: 978-0975295632)
A novel about an Iraqi refugee living in Athens who falls in love with his American cousin

The Flavor of Cultures
(ISBN-13: 978-0975295663)
A novel about a Chaldean girl in America who tries to find her individuality while maintaining her tribal lifestyle

I Am a Mute Iraqi with a Voice
(ISBN-13: 978-0975295694)
A collection of 76 poems

The Great American Family: A Story of Political Disenchantment
(ISBN-13: 978-0977679058)
Through a single case, Namou touches on a number of important issues that are robbing American families from living the American dream

Iraqi Americans: The War Generation
(ISBN-13: 978-0977679096)
A collection of 36 articles that Namou wrote over the years which paint a picture of Iraqi Americans' political and social situation and their struggles

Iraqi Americans: Witnessing a Genocide
(ISBN-13: 978-0977679072)
A nonfiction book that provides the Iraqi American view on
Iraq and the Islamic State

Iraqi Americans: The Lives of the Artists
(ISBN-13: 978-0977679010)
A book about the rich lives of 16 artists who are of
Mesopotamian descent

Healing Wisdom for a Wounded World
My Life-Changing Journey Through a Shamanic School
(Book 1)
(ISBN 978-0977679041)
Namou's memoir about her apprenticeship in a 4-year
shamanic school that is founded and run by bestselling author
and mystic Lynn Andrews

Attributions

Aside from the personal photographs, the images in this book are in the Public Domain and/or are under Creative Commons CCO and released on Pixabay.

Chapter 1: Tatiana Larina's Dream by Ivan Volkov (1891)

Chapter 2: Virgin of the Adoption by Jean Auguste Dominique Ingres (1858)

Chapter 3: Sun and Moon Flowers by George Dunlop Leslie (1890)

Chapter 15: Vintage Postcard Image

Chapter 16: Enrique Meseguer of Madrid, Spain

Chapter 18: Kristianus Kurnia of Indonesia

Chapter 19: Oberholster Venita of Brits/South Africa

Chapter 20: Ina Hall of Berlin, Germany

Chapter 26: Photo by filmmakers of *My Beloved Enemy: Iraqi American Stories*

Chapter 28: E. Dichtl of Grobenzell, Deutschland